my first
PAINTING AND COLLAGE BOOK

my first
PAINTING AND
COLLAGE
BOOK

35 fun and easy art projects for children aged 7+

Clare Youngs

CICO **kidz**

This edition published in 2018 by CICO Kidz
an imprint of Ryland Peters & Small Ltd
20–21 Jockey's Fields, London WC1R 4BW
341 E 116th St, New York, NY 10029

www.rylandpeters.com

10 9 8 7 6 5 4 3 2 1

Text © Clare Youngs 2012
Design, photography, and illustration
© CICO Books 2012

First published in 2012 as *My First Art Activity Book*

A CIP catalog record for this book is available from
the Library of Congress and the British Library.

ISBN: 978-1-78249-608-3

Printed in China

Editor: Katie Hardwicke
Series consultant: Susan Akass
Designer: Barbara Zuñiga
Photographer: Caroline Arber
Stylists: Rose Hammick, Tanya Goodwin,
and Clare Youngs
Step artworks: Rachel Boulton
Animal artworks: Hannah George

Contents

Introduction 6

Getting started 8

CHAPTER 1
PRINTING FUN 12

Funny faces 14

Elephant print T-shirt 16

Repeat pattern prints 19

Bird print 22

Fingerprint pups 26

Printed boot bags 28

Potato print gift wrap and
    notepaper 30

Bubble wrap bunting 32

Thumbprint robin 35

CHAPTER 2
INK, PAINT, PASTELS, AND MORE 38

Ink blot lion 40

Bug-eyed beasties 42

Wax resist frog & friends 45

Oil pastel owls 48

3-D cards 50

Painted pencil pot 53

Scraper art hedgehog 56

Doodle sneakers 60

Chalky rooftops 62

Ink drawing bookmark 65

CHAPTER 3
BEACH AND VACATION ART 68

Vacation journal 70

Surfboard pendants 73

Paper boats 76

Fishy plaque 80

Beach art photo block 83

Woven sandcastle flags 86

Box frame shell pictures 89

Picasso postcards 92

CHAPTER 4
COLLAGES AND PAPER PICTURES 94

Magazine mosaics 96

Tissue paper peacock 99

Abstract clip frame art 102

Torn paper pears 104

Tissue art cat 106

Cityscape collage 108

Robots 111

Chinese tiger paper cut 114

Techniques: Displaying your work 118

Techniques: Making a frame 118

Techniques: Transferring templates 120

Templates 121

Suppliers 127

Index and acknowledgments 128

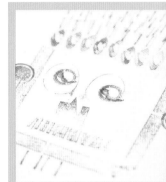

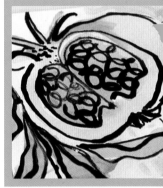

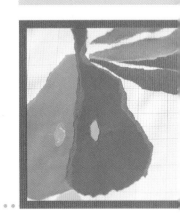

Introduction

How often have you got all your paints, brushes, papers, and pencils out and then come to a full stop because you don't know what to create? **My First Painting and Collage Book** is packed full of ideas and new techniques to try so that you won't ever be stuck again! You will find out how to use your materials in new ways to make stunning works of art.

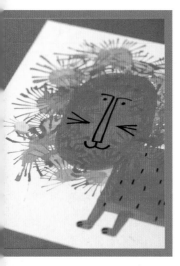

You'll discover how to make wax resist pictures, ink blot creations, and scraper art in the painting fun section. In the paper and collage chapter, make postcards to send to your friends and recycle scraps of colored paper and magazines to make amazing pictures. There are also some great ideas for adapting things like T-shirts, bags, and notebooks with your own unique designs, and you can have lots of fun with printing using materials like string and even an old pair of shoes! Many of the projects would make lovely gifts, and there are ideas for greeting cards and gift wrap, too. Your friends and family will really appreciate your hard work.

You'll find one, two, or three smiley faces at the beginning of each project. These will help you to decide how simple the project is and whether you will need any special materials or help from an adult. A guide to each smiley face is given below.

You can develop your artistic skills and practice them wherever you are, even on the beach! It is a really good idea to keep a sketchbook with you and a couple of drawing pencils. Waiting at a bus stop or sitting on a train need never be boring again. Be observant, look around you, note the way the light is falling and the shadows are forming. Look at the shape of objects and the different textures. Jot down ideas for later and never worry about making mistakes. The lovely thing about a sketchbook is that you should never need to use an eraser.

I hope this book will give you lots of ideas to experiment with techniques, develop your own ideas—and have fun! Everyone has a creative side tucked away; you just have to let it out!

Project levels

Level 1

These projects use everyday art materials and are very easy.

Level 2
These projects require some special materials.

Level 3
These projects require some special materials and help from an adult.

Getting started

It is a good idea to have a small selection of good-quality materials rather than lots of cheap, half-used, or worn-out items. Why not save up some pocket money for a nice set of pencils or paints, and add to your collection at birthdays and Christmas time? A trip to the art store can be great fun and I have made a list of supplies to help get you going on the projects in this book.

Equipment

Pencil sharpener

Erasers

Ruler

Scissors—one pair of small, sharp-pointed scissors for cutting delicate patterns and one large pair with long blades for cutting straight lines

Craft scissors with a patterned cutting edge (not essential, but nice to have)

PVA glue

Glue stick

Masking tape

Low-tack putty

Palette or plate for mixing paint

Water pot or jar

Paper towels

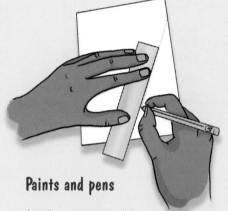

Paints and pens

Acrylic or poster paints

Watercolors (not essential, but nice to have)

Colored inks

Paintbrushes of different sizes

Colored pencils

Lead pencils—a selection from hard (2H) to soft (HB)

Oil pastels

Wax crayons

Felt-tipped pens

Fabric markers

Soluble ink stamp pads (not essential, but nice to have)

Colored chalks

Fabric paint

Air-drying modeling clay

Be safe!

* Some of the projects suggest using a craft knife. Craft knives are extremely sharp, so you should always ask an adult to do it for you. A cutting mat and a metal ruler should be used.

* Be careful when using scissors. Hold the scissors steady in one place and let your other hand move the paper around as you cut.

Paper

White and colored paper— a pad of drawing (cartridge) paper is very useful

White and colored card

Tracing paper

Foamboard

Old magazines or brochures for cutting

Colored tissue paper

Squared paper

Free materials!

• Remember to keep back anything from the recycling box that could be useful for your projects. Ask permission before you cut up newspapers and magazines!

• Keep used bits of gift wrap and ribbon.

• Cut pretty buttons from clothes that are too worn out for the thrift store and are heading for the recycling box.

• When out and about in the park or along the beach, you will be amazed at how many things you can collect and use in your art. Pretty leaves in the fall, mini pinecones, dried grasses, and acorns could all be used in the box frame project (page 89).

• Twigs and shells painted white look cute stuck around a painted cardboard frame.

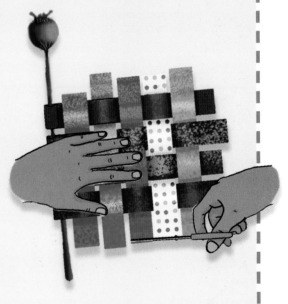

Using paints

Acrylic paint in tubes comes in lots of lovely bright colors. It is easy to use and dries quickly. Poster paint usually come in pots and is another quick-drying and non-toxic paint. You can easily mix these paints to make other colors.

To help organize your paints and mix colors, artists use a surface called a palette. You can make a palette from an old plate and use old jars or yogurt pots for your water.

Keep a roll of paper towels handy. When you change to a different color of paint, wash your brush well in water and give it a wipe with the paper towel. Change the water regularly to keep your colors bright.

Getting messy!

There is no doubt about it, getting creative and getting messy go hand in hand. Make sure that you cover your work table before you start. You can use newspaper but better still, cover the table with a wipe-down cloth that you can use again and again. Wear an apron or an old shirt that covers all!

Storing materials

Keep your art materials in a special place—a shelf is good—and store them neatly so that you can quickly find what you need when inspiration calls!

If you don't have a shelf or cabinet to use, a trolley on wheels makes good storage or even a plastic tool box, with lots of different compartments to keep you super-organized.

Use plastic containers, like ice cream cartons, to organize tubes of paint, pastels, crayons, and pencils. Label the boxes so you can see clearly where everything is.

Glass food jars in different sizes are great for storing bits and bobs, like buttons, shells, or beads. You can see clearly what you have, and they look good, too.

Stack paper neatly and keep a box supplied with recycled cereal boxes, cartons, magazines, and newspapers.

Clearing up!

When you have finished, always clear up well. Make sure all the lids are back on the paints—there is nothing more frustrating than dried-up tubes of paint! Clean your paintbrushes, wash the palette, and put them away. Stand your brushes up in a pot or jar to dry.

Throw away tiny scraps of paper, but keep bigger bits for later works of art. Store your equipment away carefully and finally wipe down the cloth or throw away the newspaper that was covering the table.

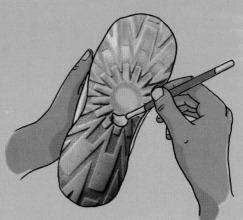

chapter 1

Printing fun

Funny faces 14   Elephant print t-shirt 16

Repeat pattern prints 19   Bird print 22

Fingerprint pups 26   Printed boot bags 28

Potato print gift wrap and notepaper 30

Bubble wrap bunting 32 Thumbprint robin 35

Funny faces

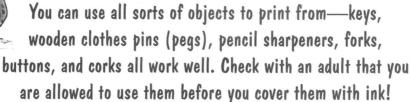

You can use all sorts of objects to print from—keys, wooden clothes pins (pegs), pencil sharpeners, forks, buttons, and corks all work well. Check with an adult that you are allowed to use them before you cover them with ink!

1 To make face pictures, start with the hair. You can use anything to print it with—forks make interesting hairstyles! Press the fork onto the ink stamp pad, then press the inked side onto the paper to print your pattern.

You will need

Objects for printing (such as buttons, fork, wooden clothes pins/pegs, pencil sharpener, cotton reels, comb, plastic bottle tops)

Ink stamp pads or a kitchen sponge cloth (one for each color) and acrylic or poster paints

Paper

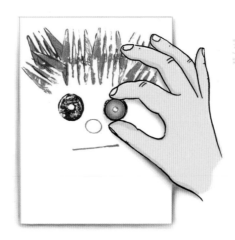

2 Choose different objects to print the eyes, nose, and mouth. Buttons or cotton reels are perfect for eyes.

Tip I have used ink stamp pads. To make your own paint pad, place a kitchen sponge cloth on a plate and let it soak up some poster or acrylic paint.

3 Use something long and thin, like half a wooden clothes pin (peg), to print the face shape and add a neck.

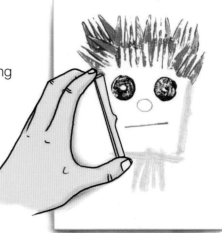

4 Finish off with a pair of weird ears—a pencil sharpener is a great shape. Choose from your selection of objects—the stranger the shape, the funnier the face!

This is a great **IDEA** for making **ANIMAL** pictures, too!

Elephant print T-shirt

Kitchen sponge cloths are great to print with. They are easy to cut into simple shapes and give your printed design a nice texture.

You will need

Template on page 121

Tracing paper

A pencil

Paper

Small scissors

A kitchen sponge cloth

A felt-tipped pen

Fabric paint and a paintbrush

A piece of card

A plain white cotton T-shirt

1 Trace the elephant template on page 121 and transfer it onto a piece of paper (see page 120). Carefully cut out the paper template around the outside of the shape, then cut out the blanket decoration in one piece and the eye.

2 Next, cut out the oval shapes from the blanket decoration. Fold the paper in half across the ovals to make it easier to cut them out. Cut carefully around the shape, keeping the paper ovals whole.

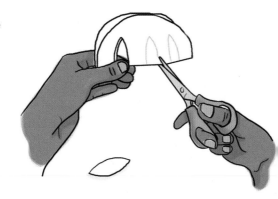

3 Lay the paper templates down on the sponge cloth, putting the elephant back together with all the pieces in the same place as the template on page 121. Draw around all the shapes with a felt-tipped pen, including the eye and the separate pieces of the decoration on the blanket, together with the windows in the oval.

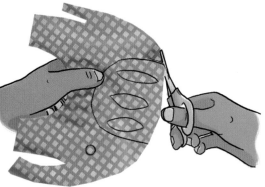

4 Cut out the sponge pieces: first cut around the elephant's body, then cut away the blanket decoration, and cut out the oval shapes. You can cut the "window" in the center, too, if you wish. Fold each cut-out oval in half, draw a half-oval shape on the fold, then cut it out. You will now have a large oval with an oval "window" in the middle. Throw away the cut-out middles.

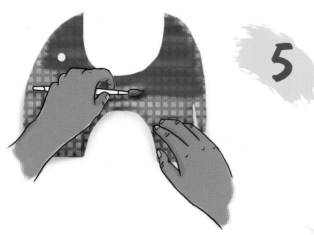

5 Now you can start to print. Begin with the main piece of the elephant. Brush one side of the sponge shape all over with fabric paint.

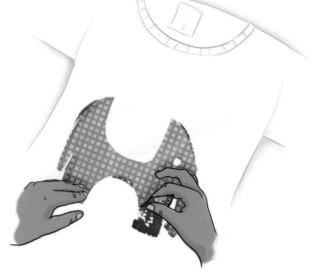

6 Insert a piece of card inside the T-shirt, to stop the paint from soaking through to the back. Lay the elephant shape paint side down, in position on the front of the white T-shirt. Press down firmly, making sure that all the different parts make contact with the fabric so that the paint transfers evenly. Peel the cloth back carefully.

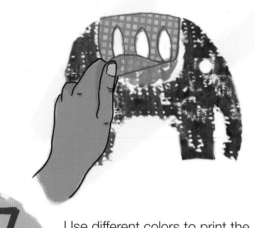

7 Use different colors to print the blanket section and then print the ovals into the space on the blanket in a contrasting color and color in the eye. Let the paint dry, then fix the paint following the manufacturer's instructions. This usually involves ironing, so ask an adult to help you.

Repeat pattern prints

A pattern printed from a design cut into a potato, or using the oblong shape of an eraser, can transform a blank piece of paper. Use your designs to wrap presents, cover files, or make this smart notebook with an elastic loop to hold it closed.

Remember to ask an adult to help you with the cutting.

You will need

A potato

A knife

A felt-tipped pen

An eraser

Ink stamp pads or paints and a sponge

A stapled notebook

A ruler

A pencil

PVA glue

Large scissors

Colored paper

A blunt-ended yarn needle

Round elastic

Sticky tape

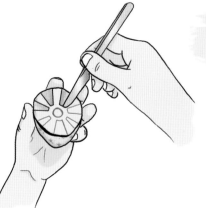

1 Ask an adult to help you cut a potato in half. Draw a pattern on the cut side of the potato with a felt-tipped pen—a simple shape, like a flower or star, will work better than something more complicated.

Carefully cut out the design, cutting away a horizontal slice of the background to a depth of about ⅛ in. (3 mm). You may need help from an adult with this.

2 Your potato is now ready to print from. You can use an ink stamp pad or make your own by placing a kitchen sponge cloth on a plate and soaking it with paint.

Press the cut side of the potato in the ink or paint and then press it onto the paper. Keep re-inking the potato and press hard to make sure that all of the shape is in contact with the paper. For a repeated pattern, line up each print carefully.

3 To make an eraser stamp, cut oblongs from erasers or draw a shape to cut out, as you did on the potato. Load with ink or paint, as in Step 2, and print your pattern. Changing the direction of the oblong will create an interesting pattern—and if you keep printing as the ink runs out, you will get lighter shades of color.

4 To make a cover for a notebook, place the notebook down on the printed paper so you can carefully draw around it to get the right size. Cut it out, and then glue it to the front of the notebook.

5 Cut a strip of colored paper that is the same width as the notebook and 3 in. (8 cm) wide. Fold it in half, mark the center on the fold, and pierce a hole through the mark with a blunt-ended yarn needle. You may need to ask an adult to help you.

6 Cut a piece of elastic that, when folded in half and stretched slightly, fits across the width of the notebook, with approx. ¾ in. (2 cm) extra for sticking down. With the elastic folded in half, poke the folded end through the hole from the back of the folded paper. Pull it through, leaving about ¾ in. (2 cm) at the end. Stick this to the inside of the folded paper with a bit of sticky tape.

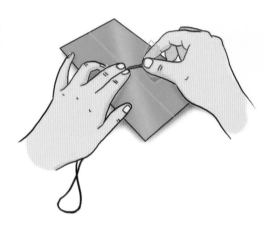

7 Apply glue to the inside of the colored paper strip and stick it over the end of the notebook, with the fold pressed up against the spine of the notebook. Press firmly or leave it under some heavy books until the glue is dry.

HOW MANY different PATTERNS can you make?

Bird print

This method of printing is simple to do. You start by making a collage from cut-up bits of cardboard. Then you roll over the card with ink, which only covers the raised collage design. You can then transfer the ink to a piece of paper, printing several copies from one inking—just like an old-fashioned printing press!

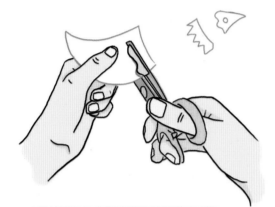

1 Trace out the bird design from the template on page 122 and transfer it onto some card (see page 120). Cut out the bird, cut off its legs, and then chop it up into sections, cutting a little from each edge in an interesting way: try wavy or zigzag edges. You could use craft scissors that create decorative edges or a hole or craft punch to make patterns. If you'd like to add more details, you can draw wings to add to your bird.

You will need

Template on page 122

Tracing paper, a pencil, and card, to make the pattern pieces

A letter size (A4) sheet of card

Large and small scissors, decorative edge craft scissors, a hole punch or craft punch

A glue stick or PVA glue

An ink roller

Printing inks in blue, green, and orange

An old plastic file or old plastic chopping board for rolling the ink

Letter size (A4) white paper for printing

Masking tape and scrap paper

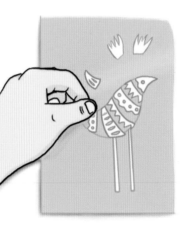

2 Use your trace to draw the outline of the bird shape onto your letter size (A4) piece of card. Glue the pieces of cut-out bird onto the bird shape to fill the space. Stick the legs in position.

3 Squeeze a blob of blue printing ink onto an old plastic file or chopping board. Roll the roller over the blob, back and forth, until the color is evenly spread out and is covering the roller with a thin, even layer of ink.

Tip You can use any card for this project—empty cereal boxes are perfect.

4 Roll the roller carefully over the raised bits of card so that the bird is evenly covered in ink.

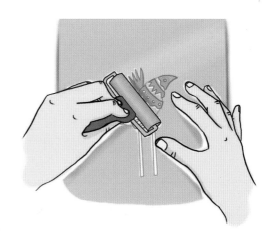

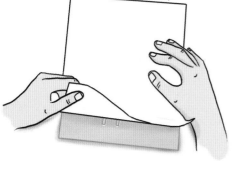

5 Place a piece of letter size (A4) paper so it lines up with all the edges of the card and fits exactly over the top. Press the paper down firmly, concentrating over the bird area. You can use the back of a spoon to rub over the design.

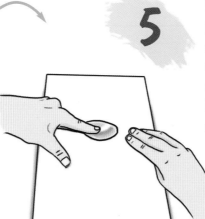

6 Carefully peel back the paper to reveal the printed design. You can print off a few sheets one after the other—the ink may start to fade a little, but this is what makes each one different!

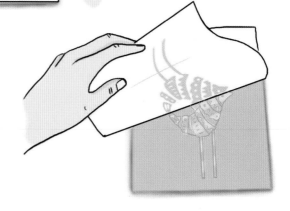

7 Wait for the ink to dry. To add the leaves and twig, draw some leaf shapes and a twig with leaves on card, then stick them onto the card picture, with the leaves at the bottom and the twig to one side of the bird. Ink the twig and leaves with green, following the method in Steps 3 and 4. You can remove the bird's legs at this stage or cover them with masking tape, so that you don't get green ink on them.

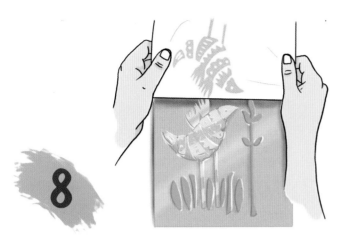

8

Print the leaves onto the printed bird paper in the same way as Step 5, making sure you place your paper with the first color on the right way round, so that the leaves print in the right place.

9

When the green is dry, cut a circle of card into a spiral shape and stick this above the bird to make the sun. It doesn't matter if the spiral breaks up a little, just stick it down—you will be amazed at how good it looks when you make a print.

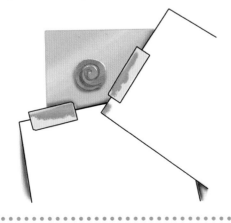

10

Print the sun in orange, in the same way as the bird and leaves in Steps 3–5. When using the roller to ink the sun, make sure that you don't get any ink on the other bits of the design. If you think you may, you can cover up the bits you don't want to print with some scraps of paper and masking tape.

Fingerprint pups

Why not paint a special portrait of your pet as a birthday card? Remember, simple shapes work the best. Look at your pet—it may have a round face and an oblong body, or lots of curly hair on a square-shaped body. Do some rough drawings first until you are happy with the shape, then get your fingers messy!

You will need

Card and large scissors

A pencil

Poster paint

A black marker pen

A soft eraser

1 To make a sausage dog card, cut a piece of card measuring 8 x 10¼ in. (20 x 26 cm). Fold it in half, so that you have a card that measures 4 x 10¼ in. (10 x 26 cm).

2 With the fold at the top, draw a long oblong shape lightly in pencil on one side of the card. Make sure you leave space all around to add the head, legs, and tail. You don't need to use a ruler—a rough shape will add to the charm!

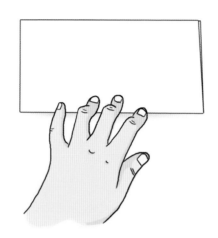

3 Mix up some paint on an old saucer. Use your fingertip to make dots and fill in the oblong shape. Go right up to the pencil line; it doesn't matter if you go over it. Let the paint dry.

4 Use a pencil to draw in a head, the feet, and, of course, a waggy tail! When you are happy with your pencil lines, go over them with a black pen. Use a soft eraser to rub out any remaining pencil lines you can see. Write your greeting inside.

Tip You can make dogs in all shapes and sizes. Try making a pink poodle with a pompom hairstyle!

Who can **RESIST** these adorable **PUPS**?

Printed boot bags

Craft stores sell plain canvas bags for decorating, but you may already have something that you could print on, like a plain T-shirt or apron. You could experiment with other prints, too. An old bicycle tire would be great: try running the tire in different directions across the bag. Bright fluorescent colors would really make the design stand out.

You will need

An old pair of sneakers or shoes

Fabric paint and a paintbrush

A canvas bag

Card or newspaper

Corrugated card and scissors
(optional)

1 Make sure that the soles of the sneakers are clean, then paint over the whole sole with fabric paint to cover the tread.

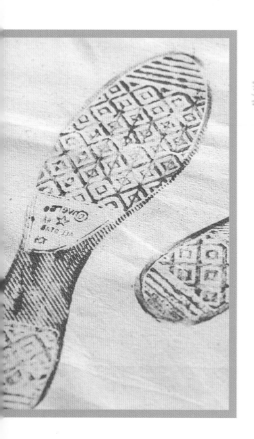

2 Lay your bag on a flat surface and put a piece of card or folded newspaper inside to stop the paint from soaking through to the back. Position the sneaker paint side down on the bag and press firmly all over to make a print.

3 Paint the other sneaker and print the other foot next to the first. If you have space, you can put one foot in front of the other, as if the shoes are walking! Wash shoes after using them to print with.

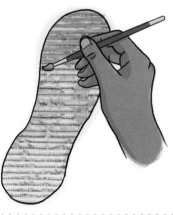

4 If you don't have a pair of sneakers that you can use, you can make some great shoe prints using corrugated card. Trace around a pair of shoes onto the card and cut them out. Paint them with fabric paint and print them as in Step 2.

Tip Sneakers with patterned soles will make your bag even cooler!

Potato print gift wrap and notepaper

Even the simplest potato print can make very stylish notepaper and gift wrap.
Use bright paper and contrasting colors to print your potato cut.

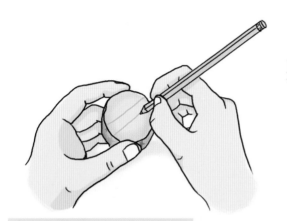

1 Cut a small potato in half (you may need to ask an adult to help you). Draw two lines across the middle of the potato about ⅜ in. (1 cm) apart.

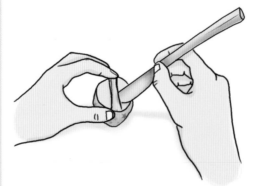

2 With a knife, make a cut about ¼ in. (5 mm) deep along one of the lines—ask an adult if you need some help. Slant the knife inward as if you are cutting one side of a "v" shape. Repeat along the second line, slanting inward to make the other side of the "v" shape. Remove the cut piece of potato.

You will need

A small potato

A knife

A pencil

A knife

Paints and a paintbrush

Tissue paper

Brightly colored paper

3 Paint the cut side of the potato and then use it to print repeat patterns across tissue paper to make pretty gift wrap.

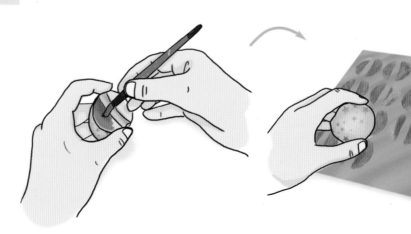

4 Clean the paint off the potato. Re-ink the potato with a different color and print a line of shapes along the top of brightly colored paper to make matching notepaper.

Tip Make a gift tag to match on a small piece of card.

Bubble wrap bunting

Whether it is to decorate a birthday party table, deck the yard for a special celebration, or simply add a splash of color to a bedroom wall, bunting always makes a cheerful display. It is very easy to make and you could add letters to spell a name or write a message.

You will need

Paper

A pencil

A ruler

Large scissors

Bubble wrap

Paint and a paintbrush

Newspaper or scrap paper

PVA glue

String

1 Fold a sheet of paper in half and cut along the fold line to make two oblongs. Mark the center point with a pencil along the bottom edge of one of the short sides. Mark a point ¾ in. (2 cm) down from the top edge on each long side of the oblong.

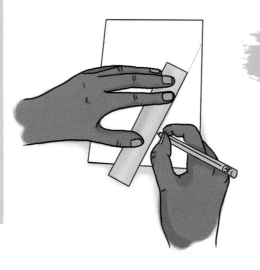

2 Use a ruler to join up one pencil mark on the side edge to the marked center point on the bottom edge. Repeat on the opposite side to make a triangle.

3 Cut along the pencil lines to make a triangle. Cut out some more triangles. To speed things up, you can use the first triangle as a template to draw around.

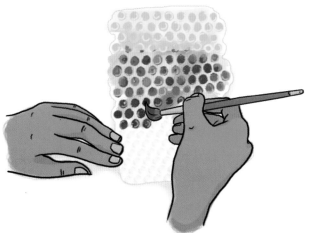

4 Cut out a section of bubble wrap slightly bigger than the paper triangle. Paint wide stripes in different colors across the bubble wrap.

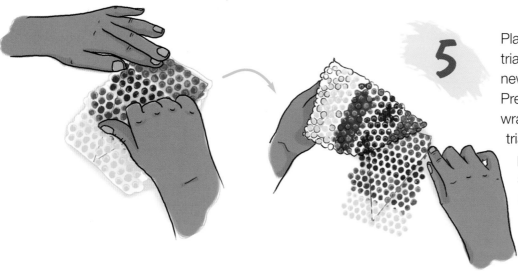

5 Place your first paper triangle on a large piece of newspaper or scrap paper. Press the painted bubble wrap down onto the paper triangle to print the pattern. Put it to one side to dry and print the next one. Keep printing, reapplying the paint when necessary.

6 When the paint is dry, turn the triangles over and print the other side. Let them dry.

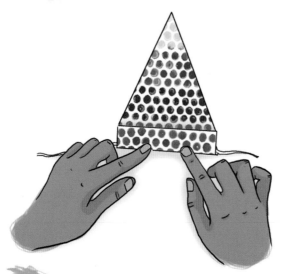

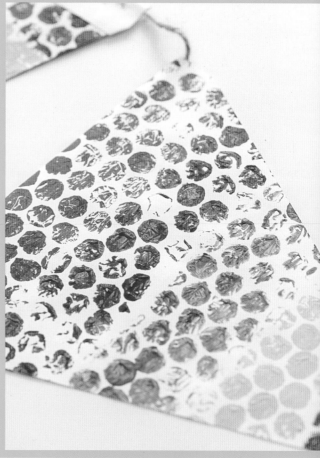

7 Fold over the top edge by ⅜ in. (1 cm). Glue along this flap and then fold it over a length of string, sandwiching the string in the fold. Keep sticking the triangles all along the length of string, leaving a small space between each flag.

The best BUNTING to BLOW in the BREEZE!

Thumbprint robin

This cute little bird would make lovely cards. The birds in a row are very quick to make. If you need a set of birthday invitations or you are making cards for your classmates, you can print up a flock of birds in no time!

You will need

Thin white card

Large and small scissors

A potato

A knife

Water-based ink stamp pad or paint in pale blue and red

Template on page 122

Thin brown cardboard or brown paper

A black felt-tipped pen

Green paper

A glue stick

1 Cut a piece of thin card measuring 12 x 6 in. (30 x 15 cm). Fold it in half so that you have a square card.

2 Follow the instructions in the potato print project on page 30 to make a potato stamp for the background, or use a stamp that you have already made. Print a background pattern in pale blue.

3 Trace the robin shape from the template on page 122 and transfer it onto some brown card or paper.

4 Draw a thick black line around the edge of the robin with a felt-tipped pen. Add the legs and an eye and then cut it out.

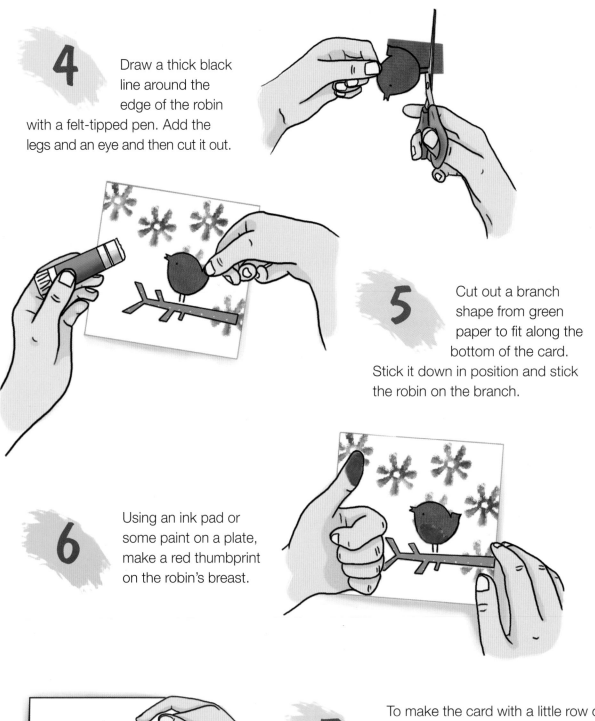

5 Cut out a branch shape from green paper to fit along the bottom of the card. Stick it down in position and stick the robin on the branch.

6 Using an ink pad or some paint on a plate, make a red thumbprint on the robin's breast.

7 To make the card with a little row of birds, make thumb and fingerprints in a row, going down in size across a piece of folded card. Draw in the beak, legs, eye, and wing with a felt-tipped pen. Easy!

TWEET TWEET, little robin, TWEET TWEET!

chapter 2
Ink, paint, pastels, and more

Ink blot lion 40   Bug-eyed beasties 42

Wax resist frog & friends 45   Oil pastel owls 48

3-D cards 50   Painted pencil pot 53

Scraper art hedgehog 56   Doodle sneakers 60

Chalky rooftops 62   Ink drawing bookmark 65

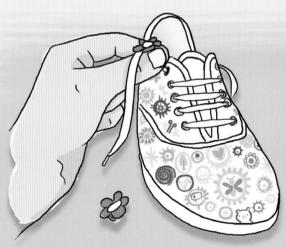

Ink blot lion

With just a straw and some ink or paints, you can create some amazing pictures. Half the fun is not knowing which way the blobs of ink will blow—you never know how your picture will turn out until it is finished!

1 To make the lion picture, paint an oval shape for the head. Add an oblong for the body, some legs, and a tail.

2 Use ink or paint—dilute it with a little water if you need to. Drop a blob of the ink or paint onto the paper next to the head. Hold the end of the straw over the blob and give it a quick blow. The ink will spread out in interesting splats!

You will need

Paper

Colored inks or paint

A paintbrush

Drinking straws

A black marker pen

Tips To make the aliens, cut out bits of green paper and blow two ink blots for the eyes.

For the hedgehog, use lots of different colors overlapping each other to make the body. Draw on a head and feet to finish.

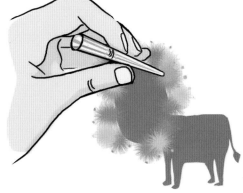

3 Keep making ink splats all around the head, using lots of reds, yellows, and oranges to make a multicolored lion's mane.

Make a whole ZOO of CRAZY CREATURES!

4 Use a black marker or felt-tipped pen to draw in the lion's face and give him some claws. You could add little curls of hair on his body, too. Look on page 118 to see how to make a frame.

Bug-eyed beasties

Use oil pastels in strong, vibrant colors to make
these beautiful beasties. With small magnets stuck to the back,
they make a creepily colorful display on your refrigerator.

You will need

Oil pastels

Paper

Small scissors

Thin card

A glue stick

Flat self-adhesive magnets

1

Choose a brightly colored oil pastel, draw a circle on paper, and then color it in. Surround the solid circle with rings of different colors. You can blend the circles into one another by rubbing with your finger, keep them separate, or scratch into the pastel to give it a nice texture—use your fingernail or a pointed object, like a pen lid. Make lots of circles in different sizes.

2

Cut the circles out—you don't have to be too neat. Stick them down on thin card in different combinations to make up the bug's body: try joining lots up in a row to make a caterpillar or join two large ones together to make bugs and beetles. Add some googly bug eyes by layering smaller circles.

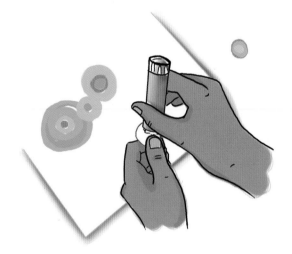

3

On a separate piece of paper, draw some curly antennae and feet—these can be really simple.

4 Cut out the feet and antennae: it is easier to cut the antennae and feet together at this stage, cutting around the outer edge of the shape. You can cut between them in the next step.

5 Stick the antennae and feet in place on your bug's body. When you have finished your bug, cut around the circles and between the antennae and feet, leaving a narrow border of card around the edges.

6 Attach a couple of flat magnets to the back of the beasties and you're ready to display them on any metal surface!

Tip You can stick your beasties on the wall, as well as using them as magnets.

SCARE your sister with a BUG-EYED BEASTIE!

Wax resist frog & friends

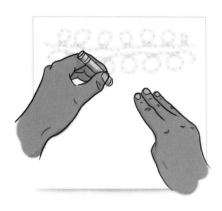

Wax and water don't mix—this is called a "resist," where the wax repels the paint, letting the colors show through. Here you can make collages by cutting up sheets of wax and paint patterns and sticking them down to make weird and wonderful animals. You can use the frog template or make up your own creatures.

1 Cover some sheets of white paper with patterns using a white oil pastel or wax crayon (we've used a yellow pastel here so that you can see the shapes).

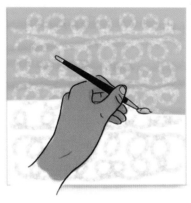

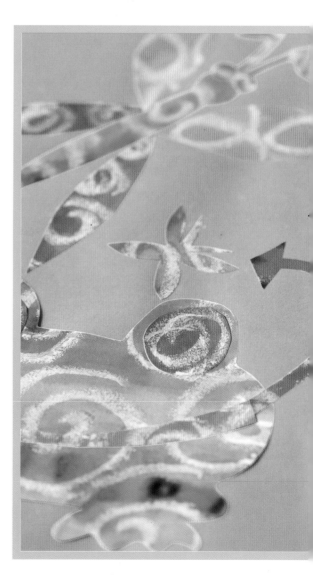

You will need

White paper

White wax crayon or oil pastel

Poster paints or acrylic paint and a paintbrush

Template on page 123

Tracing paper

A pencil

Small scissors

Colored paper or card

A glue stick

2 Dilute your paint a little to make it watery and paint over the whole sheet of patterns with a thin wash of paint. Use lots of colors on the different sheets. If you are making a frog, make sure you paint one sheet green. Let them dry.

3 Copy the frog template on page 123 onto tracing paper and then transfer the shape (see page 120) onto a sheet of the green painted pattern.

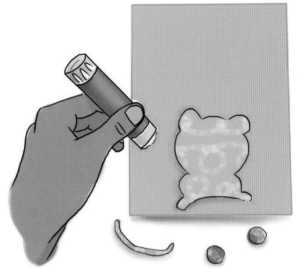

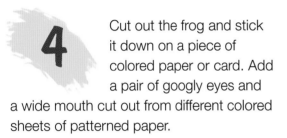

4 Cut out the frog and stick it down on a piece of colored paper or card. Add a pair of googly eyes and a wide mouth cut out from different colored sheets of patterned paper.

5 To make the butterflies, cut out a central body shape, some curly antennae, and wings from different colors. Stick them down in position above the frog. Cut out some eyes from the patterned paper.

How about making some MONSTERS or DINOSAURS, too?

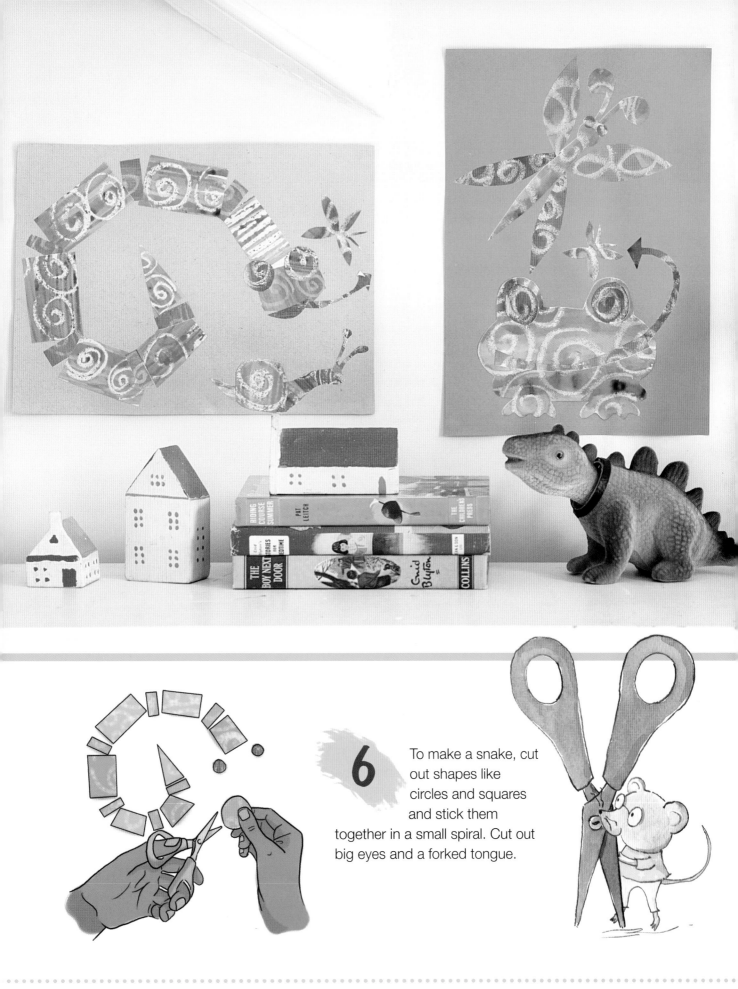

6 To make a snake, cut out shapes like circles and squares and stick them together in a small spiral. Cut out big eyes and a forked tongue.

Oil pastel owls

Using the same technique as the wax resist frog and friends on page 45, you can make this beautiful owl picture, because oil pastels repel water, just as wax does. Try layering different colors of pastels and then covering them with a wash of thin paint or ink. Experiment on scraps of paper first to see what effects you can achieve.

You will need

White paper

Oil pastels

Blue ink or poster paint and a paintbrush

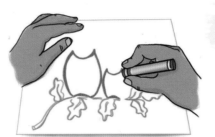

1 Put a sheet of paper down on your work surface in landscape format (with the longest side along the bottom). Using the oil pastels, draw a branch across the bottom of the paper and add some leaves. Next, draw the outline of two owls sitting on the branch—make one larger than the other.

2 Give your owls some big eyes and a beak, using two or three different colored oil pastels.

Tip To draw an owl, start with an oval shape for the body, with two points at the bottom for feet. Add two points at the top if you want your owl to have ears.

3 Color in your owls using lots of patterns and colors. With a white pastel (we have used a yellow pastel here so that you can see the shape), draw a large circle above the owls for the moon. Keep drawing round and round in the circle to make the moon.

4 Add some water to blue ink or poster paint to dilute the color so that it isn't too dark or thick, and then brush on the wash of paint to cover the whole picture completely. Let it dry.

5 Use your fingernail to scrape away some of the pastel on the owls, branch, and moon. The oil pastel colors will show up really brightly in these areas.

3-D cards

These little 3-D, stand-up pictures would make a lovely gift for your dad or grandma. Write your message on the back and they instantly become a card and gift in one!

1 Cut three pieces of card: one measuring 6 x 4 in. (15 x 10 cm), one measuring 2½ x 4 in. (6 x 10 cm), and one measuring 1¼ x 4 in. (3 x 10 cm). Paint them all over with white acrylic paint and let them dry.

2 On the large piece of card, use oil pastels to color the bottom half with a medium blue for the sea and the top half with pale blue for the sky. Add some green circles on top of the sea and then draw a whale or a boat where the sea and sky meet. Draw an orange circle in the sky for the sun.

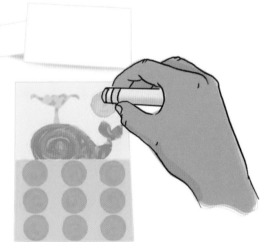

You will need

White card

Small scissors

A pencil

A ruler

White acrylic paint and a paintbrush

Oil pastels

A pointed object for scraping (like a pen lid or knitting needle)

PVA glue

3 Using a pointed object, such as a pen lid or knitting needle, scrape patterns into the waves, the sun, and the whale or boat. Add swirls in the green circles and follow the shape of the whale. You could also use your fingernails to scrape into the pastel.

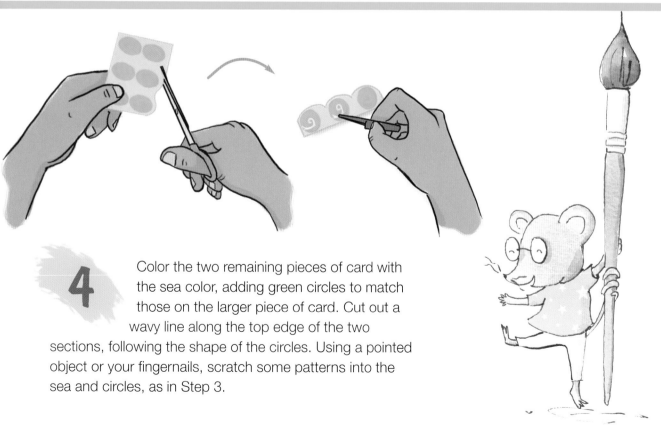

4 Color the two remaining pieces of card with the sea color, adding green circles to match those on the larger piece of card. Cut out a wavy line along the top edge of the two sections, following the shape of the circles. Using a pointed object or your fingernails, scratch some patterns into the sea and circles, as in Step 3.

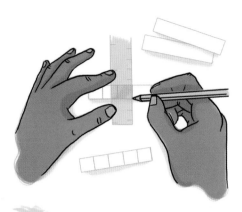

5

Cut four strips of card measuring 2½ x ½ in. (7.5 x 1.5 cm). Use a ruler to mark off every ½ in. (1.5 cm) along the strip. Draw a line across the width of the strip at each pencil mark.

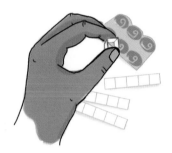

6

Fold the strip at each line. The last ½-in. (1.5-cm) square will overlap the fourth section. Glue the last section down so that you have a cube (with no sides). Repeat with the remaining three strips so that you have four little cubes.

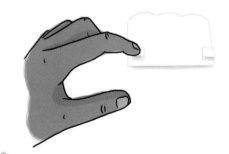

7

Glue one cube to each corner of the smaller pieces of card, on the reverse side, close to the base.

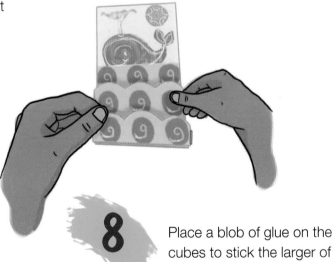

8

Place a blob of glue on the cubes to stick the larger of the wave sections to the back section, lining up the bases. Stick the second, smaller wave piece to the first wave section, making sure all the bases line up.

Painted pencil pot

Get super organized on your desk with this colorful pencil pot. You could even cover some notebooks and pencils for a matching set. They would also make a lovely gift for your friends.

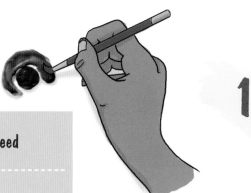

1 On a plain piece of white paper, paint a circle with a thick layer of paint and then surround it with another circle in a different color.

You will need

Thick white paper

Paints in assorted colors

A paintbrush

A blunt pencil

An empty pot or container

A ruler

Large scissors

A glue stick or PVA glue

Pencils

Tip Using just two or three colors in different combinations will make your design look very professional!

2 You need to do the next step while the paint is still wet. Place a blunt pencil in the center of the circle and pull it out to the edge of the shape. You won't see the pencil line but it will make a groove in the paint. From the same central point, draw radiating lines all through the circle.

Keep your pens organized with this **STYLISH DESK SET!**

3 Fill the piece of paper with circles of different sizes and different combinations of colors.

4 When the paint is dry, hold the piece of patterned paper so that the top of the paper lines up with the top edge of the pot that you want to cover. Mark the position of the bottom edge of the pot with a pencil.

5 In the same way, make a mark at the other end of the paper and use the ruler to draw a line joining up the two marks. Cut along the line.

6 Stick the paper to the pot, making sure that the paper goes all the way round the pot and overlaps by about ⅜ in. (1 cm).

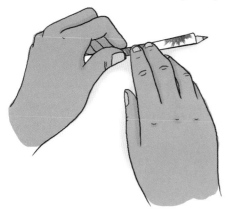

7 For a cool matching desk set, you could cover pencils using the same method.

Scraper art hedgehog

Wonderful effects can be achieved if you swap a paintbrush for something different. For this project, I have cut pieces of thick card to make a kind of comb that scrapes through the paint—ideal for lovely spiky hedgehogs!

You will need

Template on page 122

Thin brown card (a cereal box works well)

Thick card

A pencil

Small scissors

White paper

Acrylic paints in tubes

A paintbrush

PVA glue

A black felt-tipped pen

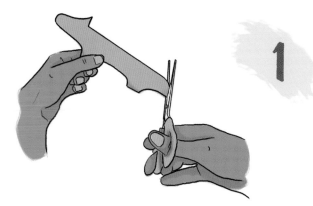

1 Trace the template on page 122 and use it to cut out the hedgehog's body from a piece of thin brown card.

2 Cut out a few oblongs from thick card, each measuring about 3 x 1½ in. (8 x 4 cm). You will need one for each paint color—that is, three or four, depending on how many colors you use in Step 5.

3 Cut out some small triangles from one short edge of each cardboard oblong to make a zigzag edge. These are your "combs" for scraping the paint.

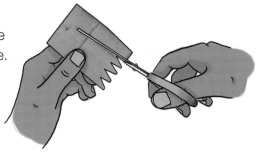

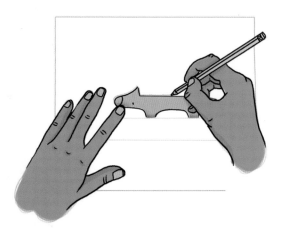

4 Draw a long oblong shape in pencil along the bottom of a sheet of white paper, a little way up from the edge. This will be the log. Position your hedgehog on the log and draw around the shape with a pencil to mark the position.

5 Squeeze some big blobs of paint along the top of the pencil line you have drawn for the hedgehog's body. Use alternate colors to get a mixed effect.

Tip: To get shades of one color, use alternate blobs of white paint and one other color in Step 5.

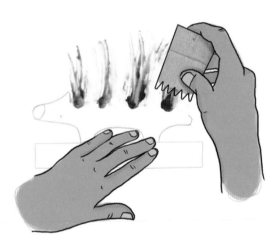

6 Use one or two of your card combs (use two if you don't want the paint to blend too much) to scrape the paint upward and outward to make the spikes.

Give SPIKE THE HEDGEHOG a wacky hairstyle!

7 For the log, paint in the oblong quite thickly, adding a couple of branches sticking out along the length.

8 Before the paint dries, drag a clean card comb along the length of the log. To make the circle part of the cut log, hold the comb and twist it round full circle, keeping it in contact with the paint.

9 Add some blobs of green paint and use the same method as you used when making the spikes to add some grass and leaves to your picture.

10 Stick the hedgehog's body down and finally draw in a black, beady eye and a little black nose to finish.

Doodle sneakers

Transform a plain white pair of sneakers into a funky fashion statement. You can buy fabric marker pens at craft stores. Start with one circle, decorate it, add another circle alongside it, and then another. It's as simple as that!

You will need

Fabric marker pens

Small round objects to draw around

A pair of white or solid-colored (plain) fabric sneakers

Decorative buttons, beads, charms, or shells to decorate (optional)

1 Using a fabric marker pen, first draw a circle on the front of the sneakers. You could use a small round object, such as a button, to make a perfect circle. Don't press too hard or the color may bleed and become fuzzy at the edges.

2 Use different-colored pens to decorate the circle. You can draw a flower or a butterfly, or try hearts, stripes, spirals, spots—anything and everything!

3 Next to the first circle, draw another circle in a different size and decorate this one. Continue drawing circles and designs or motifs in different sizes, all decorated in a variety of patterns and colors, until the whole of the sneaker is covered.

Go **DOODLE-CRAZY** on T-shirts, bags, and notebooks, too!

4 I threaded some flower-shaped buttons onto the laces to finish them off. You could also add beads, small charms, or shells. Decorate your other sneaker to match.

Chalky rooftops

This project uses a simple technique of laying chalk on its side to draw across the paper, making areas of beautiful soft colors. These colors remind me of the painted walls and shutters of the buildings in hot, Mediterranean countries—the terracotta pots, roof tiles, and bluey-black night skies.

You will need

Colored chalks

Colored paper

Large scissors

A glue stick or PVA glue

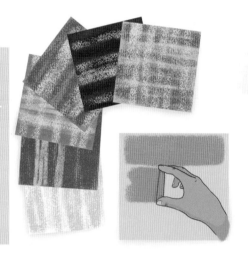

1 Using the colored chalks, draw some large areas of single color on sheets of colored paper. Try using the chalk on its side to cover a bigger area, drawing simple stripes of color in different widths. Vary the areas of color by making some stripes and square repeat patterns.

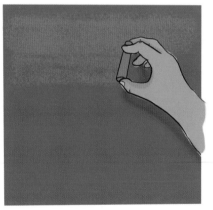

2 Cut a piece of blue paper measuring about 12 x 12 in. (30 x 30 cm) to use as your background. Use a dark purple chalk to color in the sky to about a third of the way down the square.

Tip It can be a bit dusty working with chalk; you may have to spray your work to stop it smudging. This is known as "fixing." Hair spray works well.

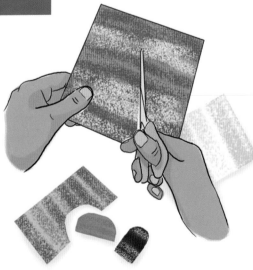

3 Cut out a variety of oblongs, squares, semicircles, triangles, and arches from the pieces of paper that you prepared in Step 1.

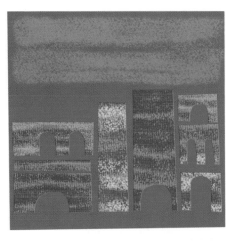

4 Stick down the cut-out oblong shapes in any combination on the square background paper to make up a row of buildings. Don't worry if the shapes do not match up—it all adds to the look of a rooftop scene. Add some semicircle shapes to make domes.

5 Cut out some strips of zigzags to decorate the buildings, add some arches as windows, and triangles for pointy roofs. Complete the scene with some flags flying from the tops of the buildings.

Ink drawing bookmark

This is a good opportunity to practice still life drawing—drawing or painting objects that have been arranged and don't move. I have drawn some pomegranates, but you could use any fruit or vegetables or a vase of flowers.

You will need

Fruit, vegetables, or flowers

Paper

A pencil

Paints and a paintbrush

A bamboo pen or quill (see steps 3–4)

Ink

Kitchen paper

Large scissors

Colored thin card

A glue stick or PVA glue

A soft eraser

1 Arrange the objects you have chosen for your still life. Practice drawing in pencil first on some white paper. Remember, if you are going to make a bookmark your picture needs to be tall and slim; the bookmark will be 2¼ x 6¼ in. (6 x 16 cm), but you can always make your drawing wider and cut it to the right size.

2 When you are happy with your drawings, you can start adding some color to your picture. Add water to the paints to make them runny and thin; this gives a nice wash effect and you will still be able to see your pencil lines.

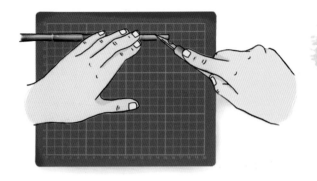

3 Do you have bamboo growing near you? If you do, you can ask an adult to make a great pen to draw with. Ask them to cut an 8-in. (20-cm) length of green bamboo and then cut a nib shape at one end of the piece of bamboo, using a craft knife on a cutting mat.

4 Lay the bamboo on the cutting mat and ask an adult to cut a slit about ¼ in. (5 mm) long on the flat, top part of the nib. You could use a feather to make a quill in the same way.

Tip It is quite easy to overload a dip pen with ink, which may cause a blot. Hold a corner of some kitchen paper in the blot to let it soak up the excess ink. Your picture may not be ruined—you could always try and turn a blot into part of your picture!

5 When the paint is dry, use your pen and ink to go over the pencil drawing. You will need to keep dipping the pen into the ink. Some lines will be thick and some thin, which all adds to the design. Soak up any ink blobs with a corner of kitchen paper (see tip).

6 To make the bookmark, cut a panel from your drawing measuring 2¼ x 6¼ in. (6 x 16 cm).

7 Cut an oblong of colored card measuring 2¾ x 7½ in. (7 x 19 cm). Stick the drawing on the colored card, leaving a ¼-in. (5-mm) gap at the top and the sides.

8 Use a soft eraser to rub out any pencil lines that you can still see.

chapter 3
Beach and vacation art

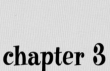

Vacation journal 70 Surfboard pendants 73

Paper boats 76 Fishy plaque 80

Beach art photo block 83

Woven sandcastle flags 86 Box frame shell pictures 89

Picasso postcards 92

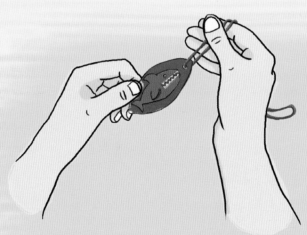

Vacation journal

Take a homemade book on vacation with you and record your adventures. You could use it as a sketchbook as well—little pictures set among the writing look lovely—or collect tickets and postcards to stick in it. When you're older, it will be a real pleasure to flip through your journal and bring back some happy memories.

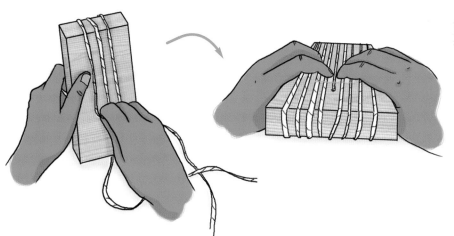

1 Use a piece of sticky tape to attach the end of a piece of string to the back of the block of timber. Wrap the string round and round lengthwise, leaving gaps in between the wraps as you wind. Secure the string with another piece of sticky tape at the back.

You will need

Sticky tape

String or twine

An oblong block of timber (wood)

Acrylic paint in different colors and a paintbrush

Two pieces of card

Large scissors

Lined or plain paper

A hole punch

Pebbles or shells (optional)

2 Paint the lines of string on the front of the block with different colors. It doesn't matter if you paint the timber a little, too.

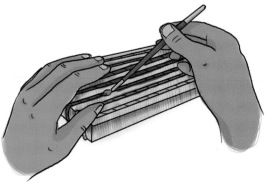

3 To make the front cover of the journal, press the block down onto a piece of card. The string will print a stripy pattern. Move the block along if necessary to cover the card with printed lines. Print another piece of card in the same way for the back cover.

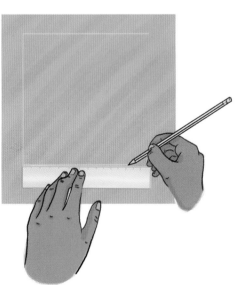

4 Measure out two 6-in. (15-cm) squares on the backs of the pieces of printed card and cut them out.

Cut out some sheets of lined or plain paper to the same size to make the inside pages.

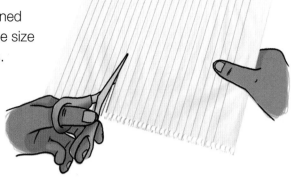

Punch some holes along one side of the covers and the pages. I have made three holes, but you can just make two if you like. If you do make three holes, make sure that all the holes line up.

Line up the covers with the pages inside. Loosely tie a short piece of string through each hole. If you have any small pebbles or shells with holes in them, they look lovely threaded onto the string.

Surfboard pendants

These cool surfboard pendants, painted in bright colors and finished with a coat of varnish for some extra shine, are really easy to make. When you are not wearing them, they will look great hanging from hooks in your bedroom.

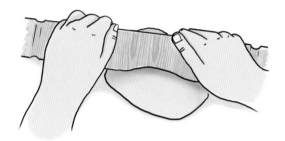

1 On a clean work surface, roll out a piece of modeling clay to a thickness of about ¼ in. (5 mm).

2 Trace the surfboard shape from the template on page 123. Transfer the shape onto a piece of thin card and cut it out.

You will need

Air-drying modeling clay

A rolling pin

Templates on page 123

Tracing paper

A pencil

Thin card

A knife

Paint and a paintbrush

Clear varnish

Ribbon or cord

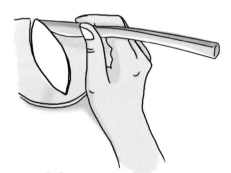

3 Put the card template on the rolled-out clay. Using a knife, carefully cut out around the template. Remove the excess clay—you can roll it out again to make another pendant. You may need to smooth the edges a little.

Perfect for your **SURFER FRIENDS** when they're carving up the waves!

 Press a pencil through the clay near the top of the surfboard to make a hole for threading the hanging loop. Let the clay dry.

5 Transfer the design from the template onto some tracing paper and then onto the dry clay surfboard (see page 120).

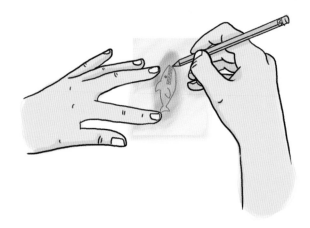

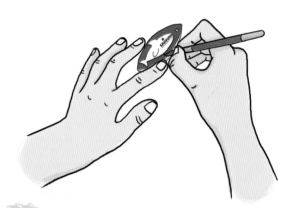

6 Carefully paint in the design. Let the paint dry before applying another color. When the design is completely dry, give it a coat of varnish. Let the pendant dry.

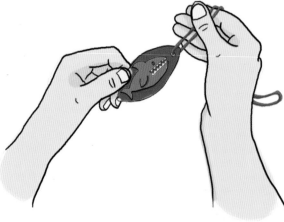

7 Thread a thin piece of ribbon or cord through the hole and tie the ends in a knot to finish your pendant.

Paper boats

These cute little ships are made from scraps of paper from a travel brochure. The paper is nice and thick and the pictures are of the sea, which makes them just right for boats. They are quite strong, so you could sail them on the water, but they would also make a lovely display on a shelf.

You will need

An old magazine or brochure

Large and small scissors

A glue stick or PVA glue

Wax crayons or oil pastels

White paper

Drinking straws

1 Remove a page from a brochure or magazine. Lay it flat on a table and fold over a strip about ½ in. (1.5 cm) wide across the width of the paper. Turn the sheet of paper over and fold back another ½ in. (1.5 cm) strip across the width, lining up the edges.

2 Keep turning the paper and making a fold each time until you have reached the end and have made a concertina, like a paper fan. Trim off any paper that is not wide enough to fold.

3 Cut an oblong measuring about 1¼ x ½ in. (3 cm x 1.5 cm) from the magazine. Hold the folded piece of paper (the hull) and pinch in the ends to flatten it. Fold the oblong in half, apply glue to the inside, and stick it over the folded end of the hull (not too tightly) to hold it together. Cut another oblong and stick it on the other end of the hull.

4 When the glue is dry, carefully ease out the concertina folds in the middle of the strip with your fingers to make a boat shape.

5 Cut out a shape from the magazine for a cabin. It can be a simple oblong, or you can add chimneys like a steam ship, or a sail. Tuck this into the folds of the boat. Use a blob of glue if it is too loose.

6 Use some wax crayons or oil pastels to make a multicolored strip of blocks of color on a piece of white paper.

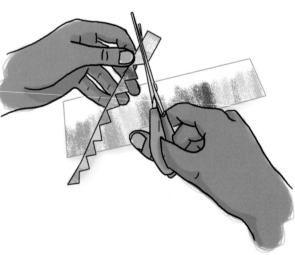

7 Cut out a strip about ⅜ in. (1 cm) wide from your multicolored paper. Cut triangles out of the strip all along the length to make some mini bunting. Make sure you don't cut right through the strip.

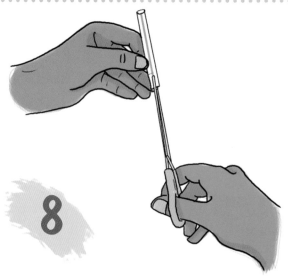

8

Cut a drinking straw in half. Flatten the end of the straw with your finger and thumb and cut a slit down the center of the straw about ⅜ in. (1 cm) long. Do the same for the other half of the straw.

9

Fix the straws in place at the ends of the boat, holding them between the folds with blobs of glue. Slot the bunting into the slits in the straws. Trim it if it is too long.

10

For a final finishing touch, cut out 2 flags from either the multicolored paper or the magazine, and slot one into the straw at each end of the boat.

Make a flotilla for **RACING IN PUDDLES** *on rainy days!*

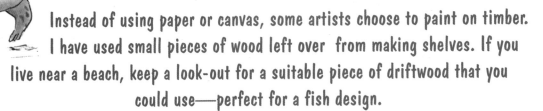

Fishy plaque

Instead of using paper or canvas, some artists choose to paint on timber. I have used small pieces of wood left over from making shelves. If you live near a beach, keep a look-out for a suitable piece of driftwood that you could use—perfect for a fish design.

1 Thin some white paint with a little water and then paint a piece of timber with a light coat, so that you can still see the grain. Let the paint dry.

You will need

White acrylic paint

A paintbrush

A piece of timber (wood)— mine were about 10 x 3½ x 1½ in. (25 x 9 x 4.5 cm) for the small one and 16½ x 3½ x 1½ in. (42 x 9 x 4.5 cm) for the longer one, but any size will do

A pencil

Colored acrylic paint

A hard oblong eraser (rubber)

A knife

Ink stamp pads in assorted colors

2 Use a pencil to draw the shape of a fish that fills the timber from one end to the other. To do this, start with a pencil mark about halfway down one side of your plaque, about ¾ in. (2 cm) in from the edge. Make another mark in the center at the other end, further in from the edge to make room to draw the tail. Join the two dots with a curve above and below to make an oval shape. Add a triangle at the end of the oval to make the tail.

3 Keeping within the pencil outline, paint the inside of the fish blue.

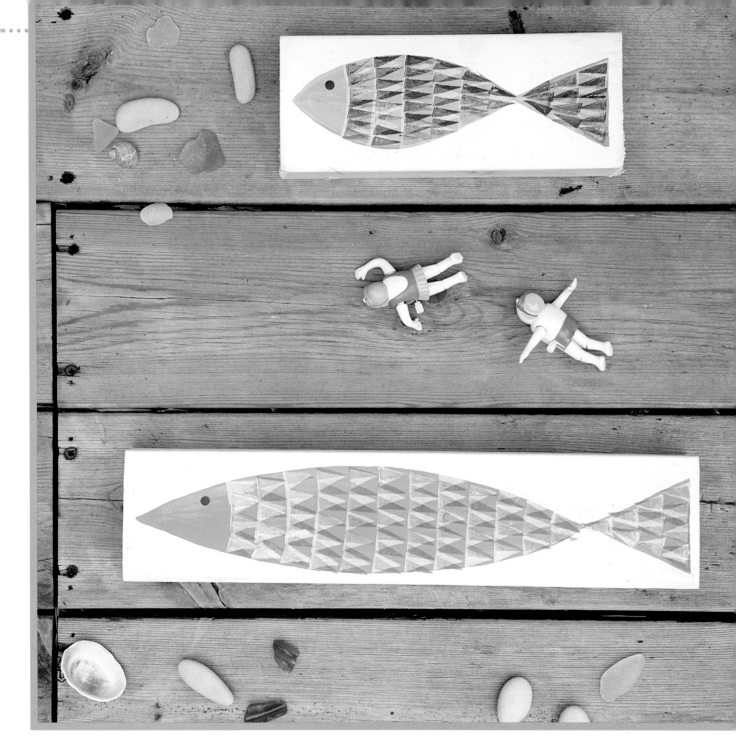

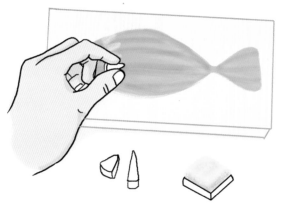

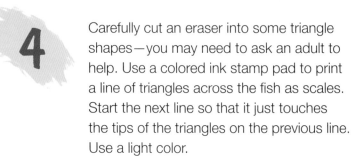

4 Carefully cut an eraser into some triangle shapes—you may need to ask an adult to help. Use a colored ink stamp pad to print a line of triangles across the fish as scales. Start the next line so that it just touches the tips of the triangles on the previous line. Use a light color.

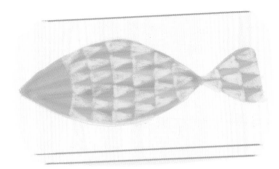

5 Continue the lines of triangles down the body of the fish. Print the triangles on the tail in the opposite direction to the triangles on the body.

6 Using a slightly thinner triangle, print a second, darker color over the first. To get a faded effect, print two or three triangles before re-inking the stamp. You can use a third, contrasting color, if you like.

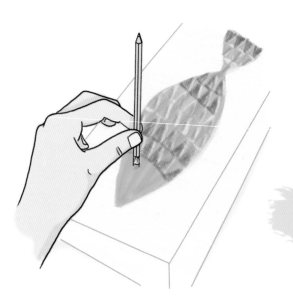

7 To print the eye, I used the eraser on the top of a pencil. Let the fish dry.

Beach art photo block

These fantastic photo blocks start life as mini works of art in the sand! Before the tide washes away your creation, capture it on camera to print out later. A few blocks grouped together would make a wonderful display and will always remind you of happy days by the sea.

You will need

At the beach:

Pebbles, shells, seaweed, feathers, driftwood

A camera

At home:

A printer

Large scissors

Thick off-cuts of timber (wood)

White acrylic paint and a paintbrush (optional)

A glue stick or PVA glue

1 At the beach, make a collection of pebbles, shells, seaweed, feathers, and bits of driftwood or old rope—anything that catches your eye.

Tip Don't worry if you're not planning a trip to the beach: photos of twigs, seed pods, flowers, and leaves in your back yard or from a trip to the park would make fantastic pictures, too.

2 Use your beachcombing finds to make patterns and pictures in the sand. Funny faces are great. Seaside-inspired pictures also make a good theme: how about a mermaid, an octopus, a shark, or a pirate ship?

3 When you are happy with your creation, take a picture of it. Make as many beach pictures as you like.

Tip To take a good picture, hold the camera steady, keep your fingers away from the lens, and make sure your shadow isn't in the picture.

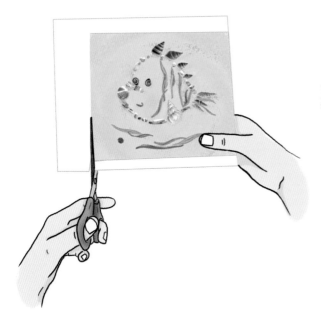

4 At home, ask permission to print out your pictures to a size that is suitable for your block of timber, using normal or photo paper. Think about making your prints in black and white. The strong contrast of light and dark areas can make very interesting images. Cut the pictures out. For a really professional effect, ask an adult to cut out the photo with a craft knife and ruler.

5 If you would like to paint your block, thin some white paint with a little water and lightly brush it on so that you can still see the grains of timber. Let it dry.

6 Glue your pictures onto the timber. You can choose to cover the whole front of the block or just stick down a small section with a border all around.

Leave your beach art to delight **WALKERS** along the **SHORE!**

Woven sandcastle flags

Make your sandcastles the prettiest on the beach with these colorful paper flags. Even if you're not planning a trip to the seaside, they would make striking decorations in your bedroom.

You will need

Colored paper in different colors or patterns

A ruler and a pencil

Large and small scissors

A glue stick

Twigs or sticks

Tip While collecting your sticks, look out for some dried seed pods on stalks–they look lovely, too.

1 Cut out 10 strips of paper about 1 in. (2.5 cm) wide and 8 in. (20 cm) long. They could all be different colors, or two colors, or a single color. You could even use some of your old paintings.

2 Lay 6 strips vertically on the table, close but not touching each other. Hold the tops of the strips down with a heavy book. Weave one of the remaining 4 strips through the vertical strips on the table. Go under one strip then over the next, then under and over, until you reach the end. Pull the strip so that about 1½ in. (3.5 cm) is sticking out on the left-hand side where the flag stick will be attached.

3 Take the next strip and weave it through— but this time start with the horizontal strip going over the vertical strip, then under the next strip (the opposite to the first strip). Again, make sure that 1½ in. (3.5 cm) is sticking out on the left-hand side.

4 Continue with the remaining strips, starting with one under, then one over. Push the strips close together.

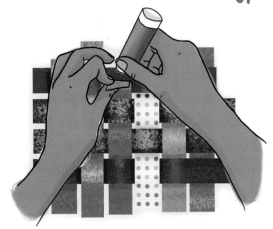

5 Remove the book from the top of the flag. Lift the loose end of the first vertical strip at the top of the flag, spread glue on the horizontal strip underneath it, and then press it down firmly to secure it. Continue all around the flag, lifting and then sticking down any loose ends of paper.

6 Turn the flag over and do the same thing on the other side, sticking down any loose pieces. Turn the flag back over.

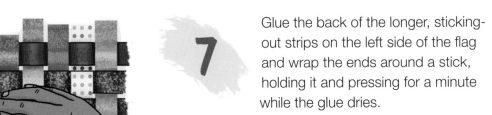

7 Glue the back of the longer, sticking-out strips on the left side of the flag and wrap the ends around a stick, holding it and pressing for a minute while the glue dries.

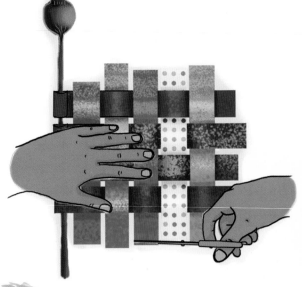

8 Trim the strips of paper that are sticking out on the edges. I think they look nice cut to different lengths.

Box frame shell pictures

When walking along the beach, I can't resist picking up one or two pretty shells. Often they get forgotten at the bottom of a pocket, only to be discovered weeks later. Now you can use a few of your favorite finds to make these cute little framed pictures.

You will need

Foamboard

A ruler and a sharp pencil

Squared paper

Large and small scissors

A glue stick or PVA glue

Corrugated card

Paint and a paintbrush

Colored paper

Shells

1 You can make your frames any size. I have made mine square but you can make yours oblong if you like. Measure out a square on some foamboard: 5½ in. (14 cm) is a good size. To make all the corners right angles you can make a template from some squared paper—for example, from a math book—or find something square to draw around.

2 Cut out the square. To make cutting out easier, you can score the lines with a sharp pencil. To do this, position the ruler along the pencil line and draw the pencil all along the line, pressing quite hard. You can press nearly all the way through the foamboard. Use scissors to cut out the square along the scored line, neatening the edges if they need it.

3 Cut another piece of foamboard exactly the same size. Use the width of a ruler as a guide to make the border of the frame. Position the ruler along one edge of your square and draw a line from one side to the other. Repeat on the other 3 sides. This will mark the square middle section of the frame.

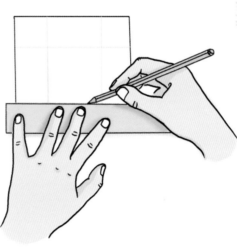

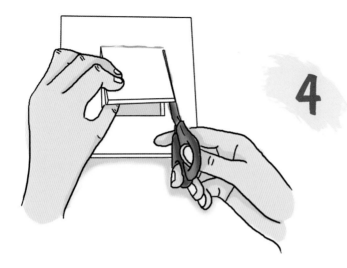

4 Cut out this middle section, using the same method as you cut out the squares—but instead of cutting in from the outer edge, you need to make a window in the center.

5 Use the frame you have just made like a template to cut out a piece of corrugated card exactly the same size and shape as the frame. Draw around the inside window and cut this out of the corrugated card, too.

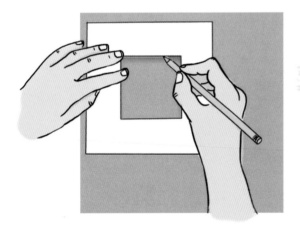

6 Now place the foamboard frame on a piece of colored paper and draw around the inside of the window. Cut out the square. You will create your artwork on this. Put it to one side while you stick the frame together.

7 Stick the foamboard frame onto the foamboard base and stick the corrugated card on top to give the frame an interesting texture. You can then paint it. I have painted my frames white, but you can paint yours any color you like.

8 Now create your artwork. Lay shells onto the colored paper and think about how you could use them in a picture. You could do the same as me and paint a fairy, a little bird, a snail, or houses, or make up your own. When you have decided, paint or draw the picture and stick it in place inside the frame. Let it dry.

9 Finally, stick the shells in position and let the picture dry.

Picasso postcards

These postcards are small collages and were inspired by one of the most well-known artists of all time, Pablo Picasso. Before starting your collage, really look at the buildings and landscape around you. Do some sketches and try to pick out a few things that would make good shapes for a collage. It may be lots of windows in a tall building or a group of interesting pots and plants.

You will need

Scraps of colored paper

A sketch from your vacation

Thin white card

A ruler

Large and small scissors

A glue stick or PVA glue

Colored pencils

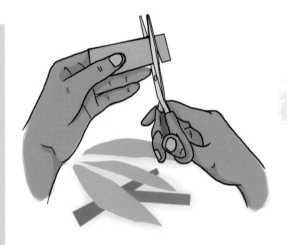

1 Gather together some scraps of colored paper. You can use bits of magazines and newspapers or packaging. Using one of your sketches as a guide, cut out some shapes of the buildings or landscape.

2 Cut out some postcards of thin white card measuring about 4 x 6 in. (10 x 15 cm).

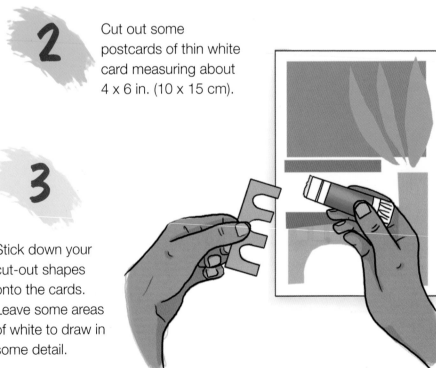

3 Stick down your cut-out shapes onto the cards. Leave some areas of white to draw in some detail.

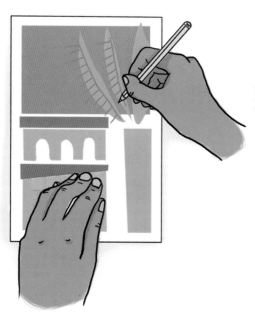

4 With some colored pencils, draw some details or patterns over the top of your collage. You could add some leaves on a tree, bricks on a building, or ripples in water. Write your message on the back and go to the mail box!

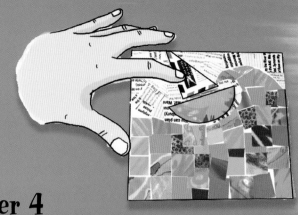

chapter 4

Collages and paper pictures

Magazine mosaics 96   Tissue paper peacock 99

Abstract clip frame art 102

Torn paper pears 104   Tissue art cat 106

Cityscape collage 108

Robots 111   Chinese tiger paper cut 114

Magazine mosaics

Mosaic is the art of creating pictures or patterns from small squares of color. It is an ancient art form and many beautiful examples have survived the centuries. Usually they are made of squares of colored glass or stone, but all you need for this colorful picture is an old magazine, some scissors, and a glue stick.

1 Cut some strips of solid-colored blue and green paper about ½–1 in. (1–2.5 cm) wide from the colored sections of a magazine. Cut the strips into squares. They do not have to be the same size, but try to keep them between ½–1 in. (1–2.5 cm) square.

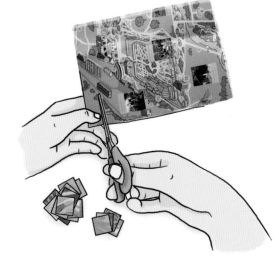

2 Draw a square freehand, about 7½ x 7½ in. (19 x 19 cm), on a sheet of white paper. About halfway up the square, draw in a big wave.

You will need

Old magazines, old envelopes, and scrap paper

Small scissors

White paper

A pencil

A glue stick

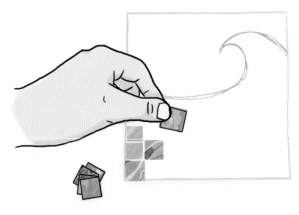

3 Start filling in the bottom half of the picture with blue and green squares for the sea. Stick down the squares to fill the space.

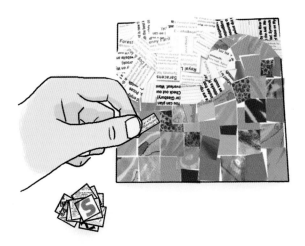

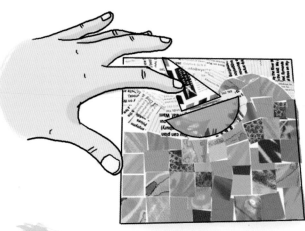

4 Cut out squares from pages with black and white words and stick these down to make up the sky.

5 Find a page with an area of orange or red and cut out a shape like an orange segment for a boat. Stick it down so it rides on the wave.

6 Cut out a thin, long triangle for the sail. I have used the edge of an airmail envelope. Stick it in place to complete the picture.

Make a MOSAIC MASTERPIECE in minutes!

Tissue paper peacock

I love using tissue paper in my art. The paper is see-through, so you can overlap two different colored tissues to make a third color. Keep overlapping to make a picture that's wonderfully rich and jewel-like.

You will need

Template on page 124

Thin card

Tissue paper in lots of colors

Small scissors

White paper

PVA glue and a paintbrush (see tip on page 101)

Card for the frame

1 Choose the color of tissue paper you want for the main body of the peacock and trace the template on page 124 directly onto it. Be careful not to tear the paper.

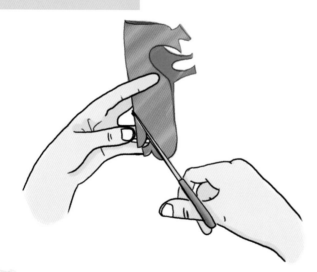

2 Gently fold the body in half along its length through the center tail section and cut out a shape on the fold in the tail. Any shapes will look nice—I have done teardrops. To cut a teardrop, cut out half an oval on the fold, making it wider at one end. When you open the fold, the whole shape is revealed.

3 To cut more shapes in the tail feathers, gently fold each tail section in half along its length and cut a shape. Continue folding and cutting the peacock's body. I have added some diamonds down the center.

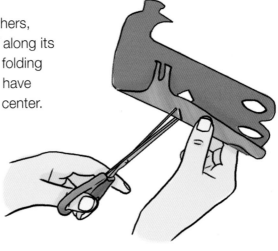

4 Have fun creating different shapes on the peacock's body. You can make folds in any direction. I added some more teardrops and a diagonal line of joined-up ovals.

5 Cut out lots of shapes in different colored tissue for decorating the body. Play around, arranging some shapes on top of the body and some underneath. Make sure you overlap a few pieces so that you can see the different layers showing through.

6 When you are happy with your arrangement, take a piece of white paper that will form the background for your peacock. Trace the outline of the main body of the peacock onto the paper with a pencil, so that you can see where to stick the other pieces of tissue paper.

7 Brush the pieces of tissue paper that are going underneath the body with a little diluted glue (see tip) and stick them in place.

Tip Don't use a glue stick for this project-you'll tear the paper! Instead, dilute some PVA glue with a little water and brush it on quickly and lightly.

8 Stick the main body back in place and then continue to add your layers of shapes. Follow the instructions on page 118 to make the frame and decorate it with cut-out bits of tissue.

Abstract clip frame art

Clip frames are not very expensive and hanging your work in groups is a striking way to display your art and transform an empty wall. Think carefully about your color combinations.

1 Use brightly colored wax crayons or oil pastels to draw rough squares of color on sheets of white paper. On each piece, start with a thin layer of pale color, holding the crayon lightly, and then build up several layers of color with darker shades on top of the lighter ones, pressing harder to get a thicker mark.

You will need

Wax crayons or oil pastels

White paper or card

A coin

A clip frame

Large and small scissors

A glue stick or PVA glue

2 Use the edge of a coin to scrape patterns into the squares of color. Experiment with wavy lines, zigzags, curves, and scribbles.

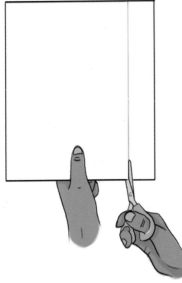

3 Measure the size of your clip frame. My frames measure 5 x 7 in. (13 x 18 cm), but you can use any size you want. Cut out some pieces of white paper or card to the same measurements as your frames or draw around the frame backing, using it as a template.

Tip You can also get some great effects by rubbing over textures like corrugated paper or string wrapped around a piece of wood.

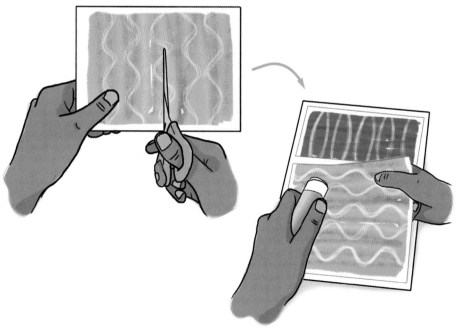

4 Use scissors to cut out different-sized oblongs from your colored squares and stick them to the white card. A combination of two colors looks effective, or cut one large rectangle. Leave a border of white paper all around, as this really shows off your artwork.

Carefully lay the card onto the frame back. Lay the glass over the top and clip the frame together. You may need help with this.

Torn paper pears

Use torn paper to make these bright, funky collages. The uneven edges and overlapping shapes make each picture very individual and full of character. You could try other fruit—slices of watermelon would be lovely.

1 Trace the template on page 125 and transfer the pear and leaf shapes onto colored paper. Use different colors for the two halves of the pear and the leaves.

2 Tear out the shapes carefully and slowly, using the pencil line as a guide. Don't worry about keeping to the lines exactly. The nice thing about torn paper art is the wavy, uneven edges.

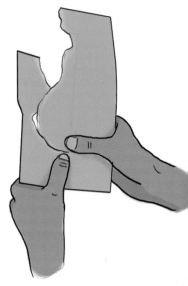

You will need

Template on page 125

A pencil

Graph paper

Colored card

A glue stick

3 To make the pip shapes, fold the pear in half widthwise, trying not to make too much of a crease. Tear out a small triangle on the fold.

Tip I have made some frames to display my artwork. See page 118 for instructions on making a frame. I have covered mine in brightly patterned tissue paper gift wrap.

4 Stick the half pear shapes down on some paper. I have used graph paper as a background as I like the contrast between the straight lines and the wavy, uneven edges of the fruit. Put some small scraps of colored paper behind the pip holes before sticking down the pear.

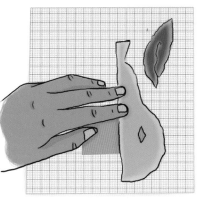

5 Stick the torn leaves in position and then tear a small triangle from a scrap of paper for the bottom piece of the core. Stick it at the base of the fruit to finish the picture.

Tissue art cat

Some types of tissue paper bleed color when wet and you can use this to great effect in your artworks to make vibrant pictures. You could make all sorts of animals—try a giraffe with squares of tissue paper rather than stripes.

1 On a large sheet of white paper, draw the outline of a cat in pencil. Give it a nice fat body so that you can cover it with lots of stripes. Draw in a happy face and some glorious whiskers.

2 Tear up strips of red, orange, and pink tissue paper. Lay one piece down on the body of the cat.

3 Brush all over the tissue paper with some clean water until the paper is soaked. Peel back the tissue to reveal the color that has transferred onto the white paper.

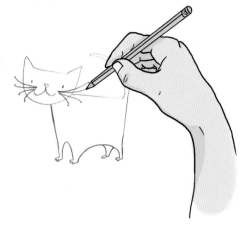

You will need

A large sheet of white paper

A pencil

Tissue paper in red, orange, pink, and yellow

A paintbrush

Small scissors

A black felt-tipped pen or black paint

4 Keep doing this all over the cat's body, making stripes of different thicknesses and colors. It doesn't matter if you overlap the stripes—the stripier, the better! Throw the pieces of soggy tissue paper away when you've finished.

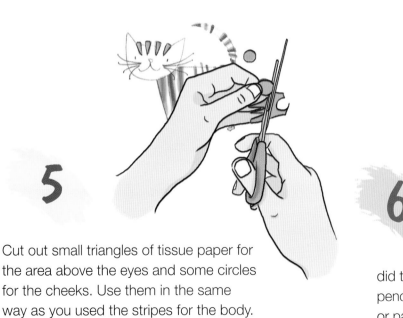

5 Cut out small triangles of tissue paper for the area above the eyes and some circles for the cheeks. Use them in the same way as you used the stripes for the body.

6 Fill in any areas on the face and body using scraps of yellow tissue paper, the same way you did the stripes. Let the cat dry. Go over the pencil lines with a strong black felt-tipped pen or paint to really make your cat stand out.

Cityscape collage

I have used bits of lettering cut out from newspapers to make some of the background to this collage. It adds a graphic element to this cityscape. The silhouette is a section of the New York skyline but any city with famous landmarks, like London or Paris, would look great, too.

You will need

Old newspapers

Colored paper

Large and small scissors

Card

A glue stick or PVA glue

Black paper

A pencil or white coloring pencil

1 Cut out square or rectangular shapes from brightly colored paper and old newspapers. The large letters and blocks of color from newspaper headlines work well. Make them into buildings with windows and cut some at angles or with pointed roofs.

2 Start arranging the blocks of color and newspaper on a sheet of card measuring 12 x 16½ in. (30 x 42 cm). You can make it smaller if you like, but remember to make the skyline smaller to fit.

3 When you are happy with your arrangement, you can stick all the pieces down on the card.

4

On a piece of black paper measuring about 9½ x 13½ in. (24 x 34 cm), draw a skyline of buildings. Tall skyscrapers look good as a contrast to the blocks of color—make sure that the buildings have gaps in between but are all attached to a larger block at their base.

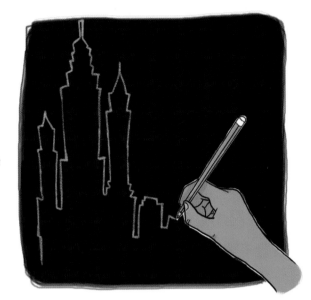

Tip If you find it difficult to see with a lead pencil when drawing on the black paper, try a white coloring pencil that is nice and sharp, instead.

5 Cut out the skyline, keeping it all in one piece, and stick it down on top of the colored background.

6 Add a few smaller buildings in bright colors on top of the black silhouette. You could also add trees and cars in the foreground.

SKYWAY TAXIS
01 785 4529

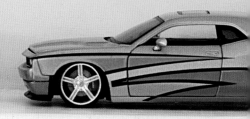

Robots

Make these colorful robots to stand guard in your bedroom. See what you can find for eyes: metal bottle tops or ring pulls work well, but watch out for sharp edges. You can add switches and knobs and buttons for some extra robotic mechanics!

You will need

Scraps of paper (candy wrappers, packaging, envelopes, old tickets, gift wrap, bottle caps, etc.)

Template on page 127

Foamboard

A sharp pencil and a ruler

Large scissors

PVA glue

1 Collect scraps of paper like candy wrappers, envelopes, old bits of gift wrap, and odds and ends for eyes.

2 Photocopy the template on page 126 at double size. Cut it out and draw around it on a piece of foamboard measuring 7 x 13 in. (18 x 33 cm)—see page 120 for instructions on how to do this.

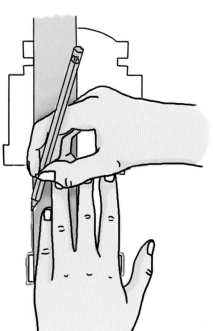

3 Use a sharp pencil and a ruler to score around the pencil lines. You can press right down into the foamboard and this will make it easy to cut out with a pair of scissors.

4 Use scissors to cut out the robot along the scored lines. Stick down your scraps of paper all over the robot shape. Trim off any bits of paper that stick over the edges.

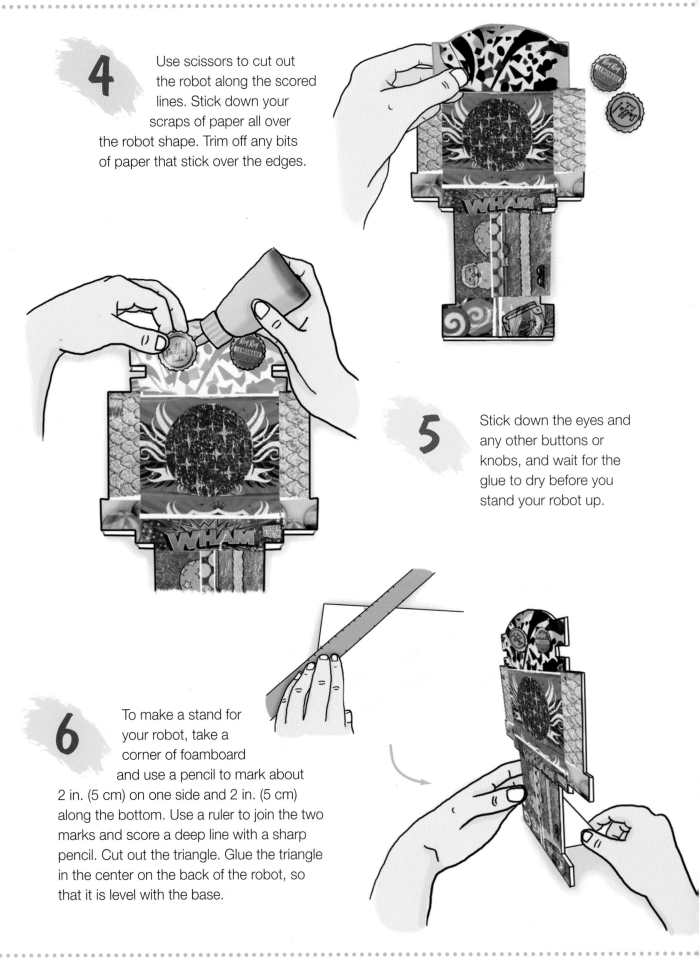

5 Stick down the eyes and any other buttons or knobs, and wait for the glue to dry before you stand your robot up.

6 To make a stand for your robot, take a corner of foamboard and use a pencil to mark about 2 in. (5 cm) on one side and 2 in. (5 cm) along the bottom. Use a ruler to join the two marks and score a deep line with a sharp pencil. Cut out the triangle. Glue the triangle in the center on the back of the robot, so that it is level with the base.

Chinese tiger paper cut

Paper cutting is the decorative art of making pictures by cutting paper with scissors. Often the paper is folded before cutting so that when it is unfolded the design is symmetrical. The first paper cuts were made in China, where paper was invented. This design is based on a Chinese tiger—not a fierce one, this one looks very friendly!

You will need

Templates on page 126

Pencil

Paper

Large and small scissors

Colored card

A glue stick or PVA glue

1 To make the tiger's head, fold a thin piece of paper measuring 6¾ x 4 in. (17 x 10 cm) in half widthwise. Trace the tiger's head from the template on page 126 and transfer it onto the folded paper (see page 120). Make sure you note which edge needs to be on the fold.

2 Cut out the shape of the head and then the features on the face. The pattern is quite fiddly but you can follow it as a general guide, making your shapes larger if you find that easier. Unfold the paper to reveal the whole head.

3 Trace the tiger's body and the patterns from the template on page 126 and transfer it onto a sheet of folded paper (see page 120). Because the paper is folded in half, the design is symmetrical—so when you open up the body, it will have 2 tails! You will need to cut off the tail on the left of the tiger's body.

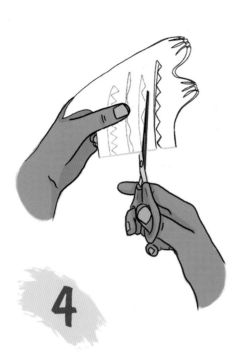

4

Fold the body in half again and cut out the patterns following the template, as in Step 2; if you prefer, you can make up your own to give your tiger some fun stripes.

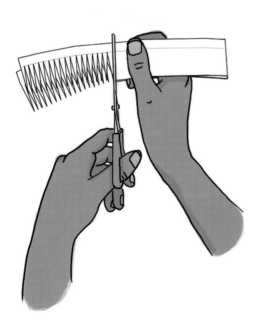

5

To make the border, cut out 2 strips of paper measuring 8¼ x 1¼ in. (21 x 3 cm) and 2 strips measuring 10½ x 1¼ in. (27 x 3 cm). Fold one of the strips in half widthwise. Cut thin triangles all along one edge, making sure you do not cut more than ¾ in. (2 cm) into the strip. It may be helpful to draw a pencil line to mark the ¾ in. (2 cm) border.

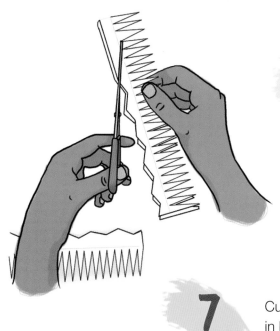

6 Now cut the top edge of the border with a row of small, wider triangles. Make sure you do not cut too close to the long thin triangles on the other edge. Repeat Steps 5 and 6 with the other 3 strips of paper.

7 Cut out 4 squares about 1¼ x 1¼ in. (3 x 3 cm). Fold these in half and make a few snips along the fold to make a pattern. Don't worry about drawing the pattern out first. It is quite nice sometimes to just cut and then see what you have when you unfold the paper. You could use a hole punch to make circles.

8 Stick the 4 corner squares into each corner of a piece of colored card measuring 11½ x 13½ in. (29 x 34 cm), positioning the squares about ⅜ in. (1 cm) in from the edges of the card. Stick the border strips in between these squares.

9 Finally, stick the body and the head down in the middle of the card. Your tiger is now ready to take pride of place on your wall!

Techniques

Displaying your work

The refrigerator is the usual spot to display works of art, but there are many other ways to make attractive displays throughout your home. We have shown you various methods you can use in this book, from corrugated card frames (see page 89) to hanging pictures with string, twine, or ribbon (see pages 27 and 107). To make your own frames, follow the instructions below.

Making a frame

Framing your work is a finishing touch that shows off your art beautifully.

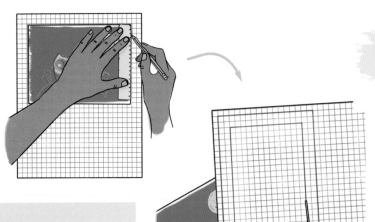

1 Put your picture on a piece of squared paper. Draw around your pictures then take it off and draw another, smaller rectangle on the squared paper with sides about ¾ in. (2 cm) inside the first rectangle. Draw along the lines of the squared paper to keep the rectangle straight. Cut out this smaller rectangle, which is the template for the inside of your frame.

You will need

A finished picture

A ruler and pencil

Squared paper

Scissors

Low-tack putty

Card for frame (a cereal box works well)

Paint and a paintbrush (or other materials for decorating)

A glue stick or masking tape

2 Use some small pieces of low-tack putty to stick the template in the center of the piece of card so that it doesn't move, making sure that you leave enough room around the edge to create a frame. Using a ruler and pencil, carefully draw around the edge of the template.

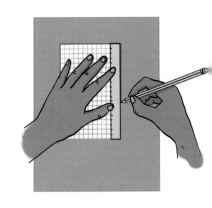

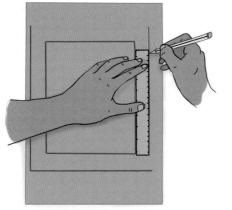

3 Use the width of a ruler to draw a frame all around your shape by lining up the ruler along the pencil line that marks each side of the shape and drawing a line along the other side of the ruler. When you have drawn a line along the length of each side, this will form your frame. To make a wider frame, double up the width of the ruler.

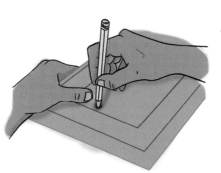

4 Cut out the middle section of the frame. You mustn't cut across the border, so carefully make a hole in the middle to start cutting from. Do this by placing a piece of low-tack putty on your work surface, put the card on top, and push a sharp pencil through the card into the clay. Insert your scissors into the hole and cut to the inner edge, where you can cut along the line to cut out the inner frame.

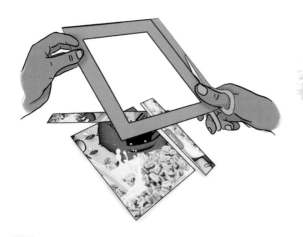

5 Now cut around the outside of the border to cut out your frame.

6 You could paint the frame by picking out one of the colors from your picture or you could decorate it with just about anything—gift wrap, tissue paper, buttons, shells, paper cut designs—have fun! Stick your picture to the back of the frame, either with glue or masking tape, if you want to use it again.

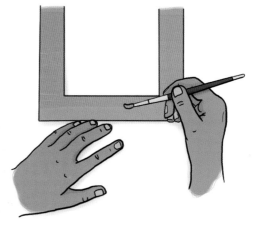

Transferring templates

For some of the projects you need to transfer the template shape onto paper or card. Some templates may have to be enlarged and the easiest way is on a photocopier—follow the percentage enlargement given with the template.

You will need

Template

Tracing paper

Pencils: hard 2 (2H), soft 2 (HB)

Paper

Masking tape

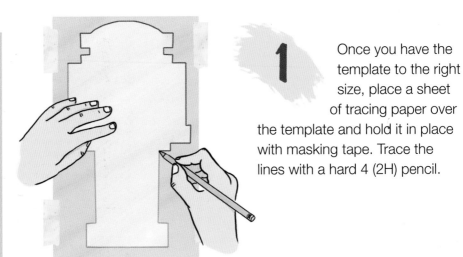

1 Once you have the template to the right size, place a sheet of tracing paper over the template and hold it in place with masking tape. Trace the lines with a hard 4 (2H) pencil.

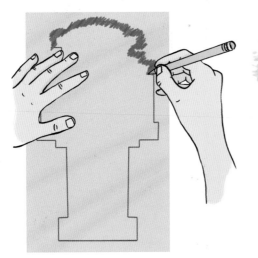

2 Turn the tracing paper over so that the back is facing you and neatly scribble over the lines with a softer pencil, such as a 2 (HB).

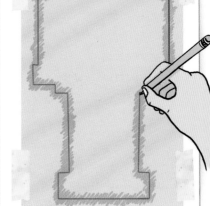

3 Turn the tracing paper over again so that the top is facing you and position it on your paper or card (use masking tape to hold it in place). Carefully draw over the lines you made in Step 1 with the hard pencil, and then remove the tracing paper. This will transfer the pencil underneath to give you a nice, clear outline.

Templates

All the templates on pages 121—126 are printed at the correct size, so you can just trace them off the page. The robot template on page 127 is printed at half the proper size—this means you need to ask an adult to help you photocopy the template at double the size, using the 200% zoom button on the photocopier.

Elephant print
T-shirt, page 16
(full size)

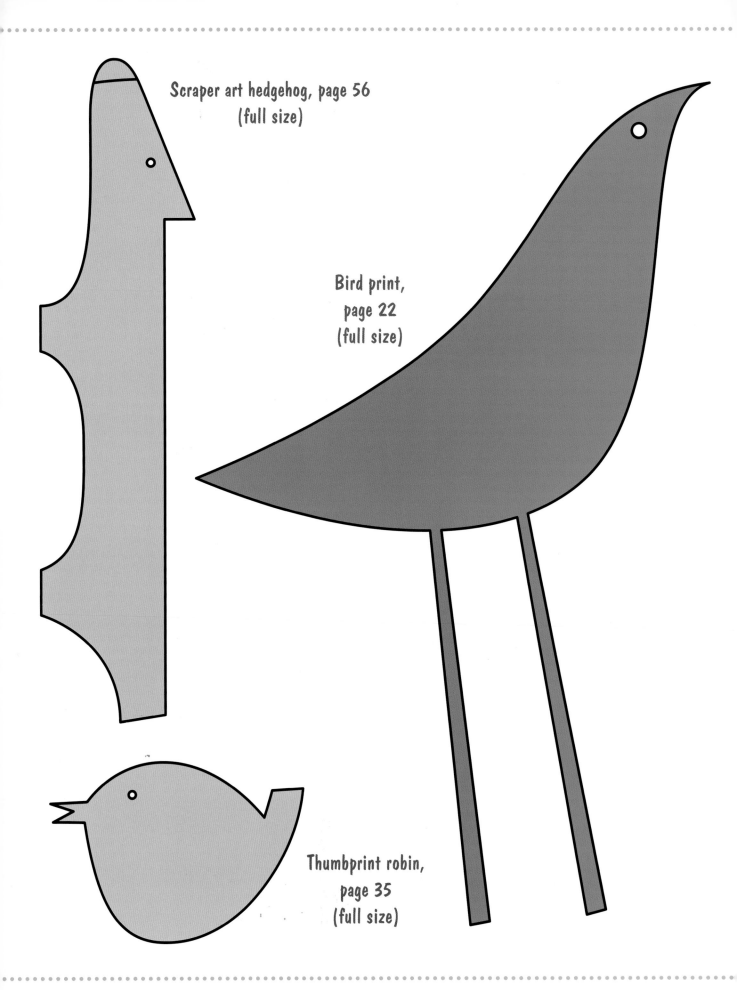

Scraper art hedgehog, page 56
(full size)

Bird print,
page 22
(full size)

Thumbprint robin,
page 35
(full size)

Wax resist frog &
friends, page 45
(full size)

Surfboard
pendants, page 73
(full size)

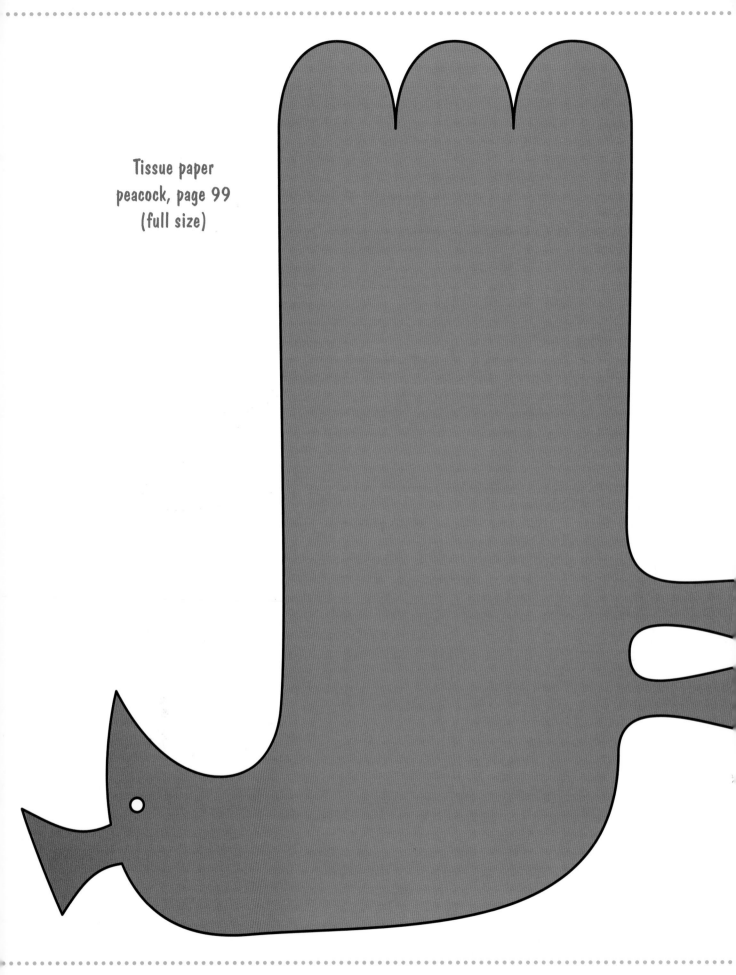

Tissue paper
peacock, page 99
(full size)

Torn paper pears, page 104
(full size)

Chinese tiger paper cut, page 114
(full size)

Place this line along the fold

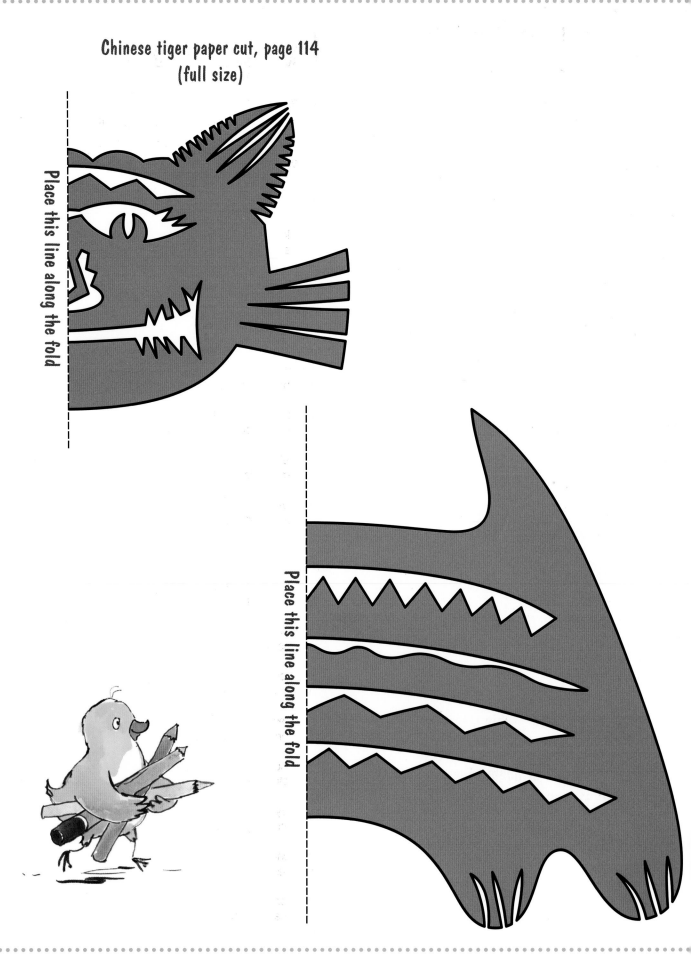

Place this line along the fold

Robots, page 111 (half size)

This template is printed at half the proper size—this means you need to ask an adult to help you photocopy it at double the size, using the 200% zoom button on the photocopier.

Suppliers

Most of the projects in this book use materials that you will already have at home, but in case you need to stock up or buy more specialist materials, you can try the following suppliers.

US

A C Moore
www.acmoore.com

Create For Less
www.createforless.com

Darice
www.darice.com

Hobby Lobby
www.hobbylobby.com

Jo-ann Fabric & Crafts
www.joann.com

Michaels
www.michaels.com

Mister Art
www.misterart.com

UK

Early Learning Centre
www.elc.co.uk

Homecrafts Direct
www.homecrafts.co.uk

Hobbycraft
www.hobbycraft.co.uk

John Lewis
www.johnlewis.co.uk

Lakeland
www.lakeland.co.uk

Mulberry Bush
www.mulberrybush.co.uk

Paperchase
www.paperchase.co.uk

The Works
www.theworks.co.uk

Index

A
abstract clip frame art 102–3

B
bags, for decorating 28
bamboo pens 66
beach art 71–93
   photo block 83–5
bird print 22–5
birds
   templates 122
   thumbprint 35–7
bookmark, ink drawing 65–7
boot bags, printed 28–9
bubble wrap printing 32–4
bug-eyed beasties 42–4
bunting, bubble wrap 32–4
butterflies, wax resist 46

C
cards
   3-D 50–2
   thumbprint 35–6
   vacation postcards 92–3
cat, tissue art 106–7
chalks 62–4
Chinese tiger paper cut
   114–17, 126
cityscape collage 108–10
clearing up 10, 11
clip frames 102–3
collage and paper pictures
   96–117
craft knives 9

D
displaying work 118
doodles 60–1

E
elephant print T-shirt 16–18,
   121

F
fabric marker pens 60
finger prints 26–7
fishy plaque 80–2
flags, woven 86–8
framed pictures 89–91
frames, making 118–19
free materials 9
   for robots 111–13
   to make beach art 83–5
frog, wax resist 45–6, 123
funny faces 14–15

G
gift wrap, potato print 30–1
glue 8, 101

H
hedgehog, scraper art 56–9,
   122
holiday journal 70–2

I
ink blot lion 40–1
ink drawings, bookmark
   65–7
ink pads 14, 19, 81
ink roller 22, 24

L
lion, ink blot 40–1

M
magazine mosaics 96–8
materials 8–9
   storing 11
   mosaic 96–8

N
notebook covers 20
notepaper, potato
print 30–1

O
oil pastels 42–4
owls 48–9
owls, wax resist 48–9

P
paints 8, 10
paper 8
paper boats 76–9
paper cutting art 114–17
paper towels 8, 10
peacock, tissue paper
   99–101, 124
pears, torn paper 104–5,
   125
pencil pot 53–5
pencils 8
   covered 55
pendants, surfboard 73–5
pens 8
   bamboo 66
   fabric marker 60
Picasso, Pablo 92
pictures, chalk 62–4
potato prints 19–20, 30–1
printing 19–37
   objects for 14
   with string 70
project levels 7
pups, fingerprint 26–7

R
repeat pattern prints 19–20
robots 111–13, 127
rooftops picture 62–4

S
safety 9
scraper art, hedgehog 56–9
shell pictures, box frame
   89–91
snake, wax resist 47
sneakers, doodle 60–1
sponge cloths 16
sprays, to fix chalk 62
storing materials 11
surfboard pendants 73–5,
   123

T
T-shirt, elephant print 16–18
techniques 118–20
templates
   birds 122
   Chinese tiger 126
   elephant 121
   enlarging 121
   frog 123

   hedgehog 122
   peacock 124
   pears 125
   robot 127
   surfboard pendants 123
   transferring to card 120
three-D cards 50–2
thumbprint birds 35–7
tissue paper
   cat 106–7
   peacock 99–101
torn paper art
   cat 106–7
   pears 104–5
tracing paper, for transferring
   templates 120
twigs 86–8

V
vacation postcards 92–3

W
wax resist 45–9
   frogs 45–6
   owls 48–9
wood, painting on 80–2

Acknowledgments

Thank you to Cindy Richards and all at CICO Books for giving me the opportunity to work on such a fun project, and a special thanks to Carmel Edmonds who kept everything running so smoothly. Thanks to Caroline Arber for her wonderful photography and Rose Hammick and Tanya Goodwin for their inspiring styling. Thanks also to Katie Hardwicke and Susan Akass for their expert editing and to Hannah George and Rachel Boulton for their lovely artworks.

As always, a special thank you to my lovely family, Ian, Milly, Florence, Henrietta, and Harvey, who all share my love of everything arty and crafty, and thanks finally to Ma Rose who bought me cups of tea and kept Otis company while I finished the book!